Dalit Agenda and Grazing Land to Scheduled Castes and Scheduled Tribes

By the same author

— Dalit and Tribal Leadership in Panchayats
— Human Rights and Poverty in India: Theoretical Issues and Empirical Evidences **(In 5 Volumes)**

About the Editor

Dr. S.N. Chaudhary a Professor of Sociology is currently Rajiv Gandhi Chair Professor at Barkatullah University, Bhopal. He is a former fellow of A.N. Sinha Institute of Social Studies, Patna; Indian Institute of Advanced Study, Shimla; and SMH, Paris. He has worked among Red Indians in British Columbia, Canada. Dr. Chaudhary has written, edited and translated 25 books and published 50 articles in professional journals. Currently, Dr. Chaudhary is working on Gains and Pains of Globalisation, Tribes and Their Indigenous Knowledge, Untouchability and Tribal Development.

Dalit Agenda and Grazing Land to Scheduled Castes and Scheduled Tribes

Edited by

S.N. Chaudhary

CONCEPT PUBLISHING COMPANY, NEW DELHI-110059

Cataloging in Publication Data—DK
Courtesy: D.K. Agencies (P) Ltd. <docinfo@dkagencies.com>

Dalit agenda and grazing land to scheduled castes and scheduled tribes / edited by S.N. Chaudhary.
p. ; cm.
Contributed articles.
With reference to Madhya Pradesh, India.
Includes bibliographical references.
Includes index.
ISBN 8180693813

1. Commons—India—Madhya Pradesh. 2. Allotment of land—India—Madhya Pradesh. 3. Land use, Rural—Government policy—India—Madhya Pradesh. 4. Dalits—Government policy—India—Madhya Pradesh. 5. Madhya Pradesh (India)—Scheduled tribes—Government policy.
I. Chaudhary, S. N. (Shyam Nandan), 1954-

DDC 333.209 543 22

ISBN - 81-8069-381-3

First Edition : 2007

Publisher
Ashok Kumar Mittal
Concept Publishing Co.
A/15-16, Commercial Block, Mohan Garden
New Delhi-110059 (India)
Tel.: 25351460, 25351794
Fax : 091-25357103
E-mail : publishing@conceptpub.com

Foreword

Land has always been considered not only an asset but even an indicator of prestige by the people, specially the rural-folk in India. The people of the marginal groups and communities have ever remained deprived of ownership of land, though they have been the most competent ones to cultivate and make it fertile for growing food grains and vegetation for others. The history of ownership of land and its shift or ownership from communitarian to private hands, drawn from few sections of population in the country, is quite old and well-known to the social science academia. In other words, land initially owned and cultivated by a community as a whole came, over a period of time, in the private hands and became private property to be inherited from one generation to the other, though it may be inferred from the system of levy or revenue on land charged by the state that the real owner of land is the state and not the private hands or individuals and their family. Whosoever is the real owner, land in reality has remained in the hands of individual who has been regarded, for centuries, the *de facto* its owner. But it has also remained confined to a few hands/families in a given village or area. So also, the holding size of land varies from 1000 acres to a few square yards, in spite of the ceiling imposed on possession of the excess land.

The undivided Madhya Pradesh occupied the largest area of land in India, though a sizeable portion of it remains covered by forest, plateau, rivers and ponds, terrains etc. even today after coming of Chhattisgarh state out of the state of Madhya Pradesh. Incidentally, the present Madhya Pradesh is a conglomeration of a number of erstwhile princely sates and their feudatories existed in the forms of jagirdars, jamindars etc., who had acquired and controlled huge amount of land, resulting into large population being either rentiers and share-croppers or landless agricultural workers.

This latter ones include huge majority of the Dalits and the Adivasis or the Scheduled Castes and the Scheduled Tribes, representing 16.40 per cent and 19.94 per cent respectively in the State, though their percentages vary from region to region. As Madhya Pradesh has remained one of the educationally and economically backward states in the country, this is glaringly reflected through the low, rather lowest, level of literacy and educational achievement as well as poor economic condition of the Dalits and Adivasis there. Their vulnerable socio-economic condition is also clear from a large number of atrocities inflicted on them by the upper and backward classes or castes over all these years, besides the continued enigma of traditional superordinate and subordinate types of relationship between them and people of the other castes and communities.

To deal with the above mentioned problems of the Dalits and the Adivasis especially their landlessness in the state, the Government in Madhya Pradesh enacted a couple of legislations soon after independence of the country. These were the Jamindari Abolition Act, 1951 and the Jagirdari Abolition Act, 1951. Although both the Acts intended to abolish the titles of the Jamindars or landlords and Jagirdars who had excessive land under their possession and control but in reality never cultivated in on their own, these Acts has far reaching consequences for the Dalits and the Adivasis of the state. But the land continued to remain, in one way or the other, in their possession. Then followed the Madhya Pradesh Ceiling on Agricultural Holdings Act, 1960, which was further amended in 1972, with the aim of reducing the size of landholding per individual or person/family and distributing the surplus land among the landless people. But hardly land became surplus as it was transferred by the owner to their kith and kins and other fictitious names. Interestingly, all the three Acts were adopted in the ambit of land reform, but there was hardly any reform in the land by making it more fertile and cultivable, specially through providing proper and adequate irrigation facility. It proved to be merely a transfer of hands over ownership on land, which had never reached to the hands of the Dalits and the Adivasis, but certainly some of it to that of the middle level castes.

Then, the government in the state had also earmarked certain portion of land for the public uses such as *Charnoi* (grazing), manure pits and skinning ground, play grounds, schools, lanes, drains etc. in and around every village and town. During the 1990s, it had reduced the *Charnoi* land area from 7.5 per cent to 5.0 per cent, with the view of distributing the available 2.5 per cent land among the landless Dalits and Adivasis, but this effort also could not solve their problem of landlessness as a sizeable number of them still remained landless. Besides, of those who were allotted land through giving them paper could not get actual possession of it. Subsequently, the area of the *Charnoi* land was further reduced from 5.0 per cent to 2.0 per cent, with the objective of distributing the available 3.0 per cent land among the remaining landless amongst the Dalits and Adivasis in the state. It is interesting to mention here that during all these years, no effort was made by the government to reduce the size of holding of the cultivable land or agricultural land owned by the persons/families since the first ceiling imposed in 1960. A policy for distributing the available 3.0 per cent *Charnoi* land was adopted by the state government, with great fan-fare, in 2002 in the form of *Dalit Agenda* or *Bhopal Declaration,* which was considered to be a model for other states in the country. In fact, the *Dalit Agenda* was publically discussed and then adopted in the Bhopal Conference held during January 12-13, 2002, which I had also witnessed as the Director General of Dr. Ambedkar National Institute of Social Sciences, Mhow (now Dr. Ambedkar Nagar), Indore, Madhya Pradesh. Inclusive of 21 issues or themes, the *Dalit Agenda* emphasized the distribution of land (3.0 per cent available *Charnoi* land) among the landless Dalits and Adivasis and the same was done within less than two months time, of course on paper or through *pattas* carrying names of both husband and wife. Whether they got the actual possession of the allotted land and started cultivation on it without any resistance from the upper and middle castes is a mute question to be enquired into. Yet, the *Dalit Agenda* as such was considered to be an effective step towards empowerment of the Dalits and the Adivasis of the State.

In the present book, consisting of three case studies, addressing the issue of distribution of the *Charnoi* land among the Dalits and the Adivasis of the state, efforts have been made to record the state of affairs at both the micro and macro levels. One would have certainly wished to have the actual account of the entire exercise either through extensive interviews or detailed narratives of the real beneficiaries/would-be beneficiaries of the state's commendable efforts to empower the ostricised and marginal section of the population. This perhaps would require another academic venture. The present book, however, is a commendable effort for which both its authors and editor deserve to be applauded. I am certain that it would be received by its readers in the right spirit.

Nandu Ram
Dr. Ambedkar Chair Professor
of Sociology
Jawaharlal Nehru University
New Delhi

October 29, 2006

Preface

Dalits and tribes constitute about 16 and 20 per cent population in Madhya Pradesh respectively. Demographically they are unevenly distributed in the province with having highest concentration of dalits in Datia district (24.7%) and the lowest in Jhabua district (3.1%) respectively. In spite of their significant contribution in the development of M.P. society in particular they have very limited access to and control over the achieved resources of power and livelihood. In terms of literacy and education, ownership of land and water based resources, health facility, possession of household and agricultural assets, proper economic income on sustained basis etc.; they are deprived and underdeveloped. Historically they are the victims of religion and caste or what may be termed as social structure based exploitation, deprivation, marginalisation, and physical isolation which have contributed to their under- development on sustained basis. Of course, one can see the role of institutional intervention, dalit and tribal movement and NGO in their development but in spite of such efforts partly because of capitalistic model of development and partly due to near absence of political and social will these efforts did not bring substantial improvement in the physical and social quality of life of majority of tribals and dalits particularly those living in the rural and forest areas.

Bhopal Declaration popularly known as **Dalit Agenda,** prepared by the Government of Madhya Pradesh under the direction of large number of dalit and non-dalit scholars dealing with dalit and tribal questions, bureaucrats, media persons and politicians, is one of the recent efforts on the part of the State Government of Madhya Pradesh to bring empowerment and development in the life condition and chances of cross-section of dalit and tribal population. The **Bhopal Declaration** dated April 14, 2002 covers 21 point-agenda for the empowerment of dalit/tribal population. However, land to the landless and near landless dalit and tribal population fall under the first agenda. In the light of this declaration thousands of acres of land have been distributed among poor dalits and tribals living in the villages during limited time period. Do the *Charnoi* land was distributed among the needy? Do they easily received both land paper and land possession? Besides land what other inputs they received? How this project have affected inter-caste relation? What are its socio-political implications? How it has influenced their economy? These are some of the specific issues which have been covered in all the three studies edited in this volume.

I am thankful to the following for their help, encouragement and cooperation to edit this volume.

At the very outset I express my deep sense of gratitude to Dr. Amar Singh (IAS) the then Secretary to the Chief Minister, Madhya Pradesh and currently Joint Secretary, Government of India who encouraged me to conduct sociological study on **Dalit Agenda**.

I am thankful to Prof. Nandu Ram, Ambedkar Chair Professor, Jawaharlal Nehru University, New Delhi who discussed with me the philosophy of Dalit agenda and kindly wrote foreword of this volume.

I express my thanks to Prof. Y.G. Joshi and Dr. Yogesh Kumar who brought out article from their studies on *Charnoi* land for this volume.

Last but not the least I am obliged to Shri Ashok Kumar Mittal of Concept Publishing Company, New Delhi for publishing this book.

S. N. Chaudhary

Contents

1
Introduction

– S. N. Chaudhary

Dalits known by different names and surnames constitute about 16 per cent population in Madhya Pradesh. However, from among scheduled castes *Chamar,* constitute about 7 per cent population (1931 Census) and therefore, they are numerically superior. If we see district and cultural zone-wise population of SC in M.P. it is observed that in *Malwa* region particularly in the districts of *Ujjain* and *Shajapur* they constitute more than 22 per cent population, in *Chambal* in almost all the 7 districts their population is more than 17 per cent and in Datia it is around 25 per cent. Similarly in the districts of Bundelkhand also they are more than 20 per cent. In Sehore, they constitute about 20 per cent population. In spite of their significant presence in large number of districts in Madhya Pradesh they are underdeveloped and deprived in terms of their presence in education, bureaucracy, business and social life. This is primarily because of century old caste based social and psychological deprivation and discrimination which they have experienced since long. They are associated with land in villages but not as farmer rather in most of the cases as wage earner and small land owner. It is needless to mention that while majority of the big landowners are mainly from the upper castes and upper backward classes and the agricultural workers are largely dalits and tribals (Sankaran, 1996). According to the 1991 Census, 64 per cent dalits are the agricultural labourers who do not have land and therefore, they have to work as unregistered sharecroppers, unrecognised temporary tenants and agricultural labourers for subsistance without any security. The National Sample Survey (NSS, 1992) reported that 13.34 per cent dalits are absolute landless in India. According to the Ninth Draft Plan Paper, the majority of Dalits (77%) are either absolute landless or mere landless (Ninth

Five Year Plan Draft 1997-2002, Vol. II, p. 347). According to Agricultural Census Report (1990-91) around 87 per cent of the dalits at the national level belong to the category of small and marginal farmers. Many of them do not have even homestead land and they have constructed huts on others land. Their women are subject to sexual exploitation and murder. According to one observation in Madhya Pradesh during 1995 alone 4845 and 4872 dalit women were murdered and raped respectively (R.A. Gautam and K. Prasad, 2001, pp. 103-04). In Sehore district 60 and 115 dalit women were murdered and raped during the above year respectively (Gautam and Prasad, *op.cit.*). Children do not attend schools. Maximum number of child labour comes from this category. These children work in the unorganised sectors in both rural and urban areas. In terms of health also their condition is pitiable. It is reported that at the national level also infant and child mortality rate is much higher among dalits incomparison to other social groups. This is clear from Table 1.1.

Table 1.1 : Health Status of the Socially Marginalised Groups (1999)

	Infant Mortality/ 1000	*Under 5 Mortality/ 1000*	*% Children Under Weight*
India	70.0	94.9	47.0
Scheduled Castes	83.0	119.3	53.5
Scheduled Tribes	84.2	126.6	55.9
Other Disadvantaged	76.0	103.1	47.3
Others	61.8	82.6	41.1

Source: Draft National Health Policy, 2001.

Many of the dalit families are the victims of chronic poverty. As a result, their entire effort is directed to arrangement of two times meal. They do not have resources to invest for development. In fact their entire time and energy revolve around fulfilment of basic need. The process of formation of social capital is unsatisfactory among them. They are not paid as per Minimum Wages

Acts. Since they are away from education, therefore, the door of job and education based activities are nearly closed for them. Of course, there is reservation facility but majority of the dalits specifically those who are poor, illiterate and live in villages, they are away from this package. Generally, it is observed that fruits of reservation in admission and job are availed by relatively rich and prosperous sections of dalit population, most of whom live in urban areas. Of course, there are some social organizations and social movements directed to the empowerment of resourceless dalit population in M.P. like *Bachpan Bachao Andolan, Narmada Bachao Andolan, Ekta Parished, Samarthan, UNICEF, Action-Aid, DANIDA, Gramin Khetihar Majdoor Sangathan* etc., but its area of operation is limited and local. Such organizations can only create and produce models but cannot bring radical change in the entire society because of their own limitations and limited resource base.

In the last one decade because of 73rd and 74th Constitutional Amendments there is facility of reservation for dalits at all the three levels of Panchayat and urban bodies as per their population size in that particular locality and because of this thousands of panchayat representatives can be seen from this category. But partly because of procedural constraint, their new exposure to formal political system and partly because of their dependence on others they have yet to address dalit specific problems. But in spite of this one can see the process of elite formation among different sub-castes of dalit in M.P. The role of seasonal out migration, development schemes, NGO intervention etc., are significant in this context.

But so far as dalits who are either landless or who possess small amount of degraded land which are incapable to ensure food security is a serious concern for all those addressing the problem of poor dalits.

Land Reform in M.P.: Historical Overview

Through Zaminidari Abolition Act (No. B of 1951) and the abolition of the Jagir Act, 1951, intermediary system was abolished in Madhya Pradesh. And in order to bring uniformity in the revenue system the M.P. Land Revenue Code, 1959 was introduced in 1959 which became effective from October 2, 1959. It included most of the traits of land reform, viz. uniformity of tenures, protection of tenants against arbitrary ejection, conferment of rights of *bhumiswamy* to tillers etc. The Code constructed only one class of tenure holders, viz. *Bhumiswamy* (land owners). Occupancy rights of the tenants were also protected and with the abolition of intermediaries (Zamindari system) the estates owned by these people, viz. tanks, ponds, water channels, wastelands, community lands, village forests, mines etc. were not vested with the state government.

Besides the above step, in the direction of the Planning Commission, Government of India, the Government of M.P. passed the M.P. Ceiling on Agricultural Holdings Act in 1960 and introduced it in November 1961. According to this Act a person could hold 10.12 standard hec. of land in irrigated areas, 20.24 in partially irrigated areas and 30.35 hec. in non-irrigated areas. However, joint farming bodies constituted by wage labour, landless and displaced were exempted from this limitation. Some extra concession and exemption was provided in the name of cattle breeding, dairy farming, wool raising, mechanised farming, orchards/groves commercial activities, educational activities and so on. As a result, thousands of hectares of land were managed and manipulated by the ex-zamindars and big landowners. It is reported that businessmen acquired ceiling free land for industrial purpose and converted the land into flourishing farm (NCAS and EP *op.cit.*). The provision of the Ceiling Act of 1960 also contributed to illegal transfer of surplus land to escape ceiling provision. The governing elites not only lacked political will to introduce the provision but also many of them became direct party to it. For example, when G.N. Singh became the Chief Minister of M.P. in 1967-69 he transferred his entire 524 acres of land to his sons and relatives and became himself landless. Many of the MLAs and MPs followed the same path (*Mainstream*, May 6, 1972:17).

Planning Commission, Government of India, conducted impact study of the Land Ceiling Act, 1960. It observed that the records maintained by the revenue department were inconsistent, inaccurate and contained errors. The *Patwaris* in collusion with big landlords did not report excess surplus land retained by the big landlords.

Further, there were inconsistencies in the estimation of surplus land, acquisition of surplus land and distribution of surplus land (*Kurukeshtra,* October 1986: 59-63).

During 1973 the then Chief Minister of M.P. Mr. P.C. Sethi took firm stand which led to revision of the M.P. Agricultural Land Ceiling Act, 1960. This is known as Amendment Act of 1972. According to this Act a family consisting of 5 members (husband, wife and their minor children) can possess upto 15 acres of land and if the size of the family is beyond 5 it will possess upto 18 acres of land. Through this revised Act of 1972 all exemptions given in the Ceiling Act, except the religious and charitable bodies, were removed. Of courses the revised Act of 1972 was far better in a comparison to the 1960 Act but it was also misused by the influentials. It did not stop fictitious transfer of land. Several thousand acres of land were sold and resoled down, gifted to religious bodies (*Mainstream*, May 6, 1972: 17-19). Failure of this revised Act of 1972 was one of the reasons for enactment of M.P. Ceiling on Agricultural Holding Act in 1974. This Act said that the maximum land that could be held by a family was 10 acres for two crops of irrigated land and upto 54 acres in the case of dry land. But this Act also exempted private/pubic companies, societies registered under the M.P. Societies Act and Cooperative Societies Act. Traders and industrialists also received exemptions. As a result, this Act was also misused and it did not bring land reform. The study conducted by Lal Bahadur Shastri Academy of Administration in 1980 said that big landowners belonging to upper castes had not been covered by the ceiling limit. Absentee landlords continued to control vast tracts of land in villages. At the state level 69.1 per cent of the owners of surplus land had land in village of their residence and 30.9 per cent of them had land in other villages. The study attributed that combination of factors like indifference on the part of administration, lack of political will and misuse of law and legal system led to near failure of this Act (LBSNAA, 2002: 107-115).

The role of *Sarvodaya* Movement is also not upto the mark in the distribution of surplus land in M.P. Up to 1994, 1,39,642 lakh hectares of land, which was only 0.63 per cent of the operated area, had been declared as surplus land. The Government could take possession of 1,13,798 lakh hectares and it could actually distributed only 74,951 lakh hectares, or around 50 per cent of the declared surplus land among the scheduled castes and scheduled tribes.

Land to Dalits and Tribes : Myths and Reality

As stated, many of the dalits and tribes were allotted land and relevant papers were also handed over to them in time but many of them did not get possession of land. In many cases the beneficiaries did not even know where their land is located, some villages even lacked village map. In many cases without acquiring surplus land from the big landowners it were allotted to the poor. The *Patwaris* and police etc., sided the landlords. As a result, the poor dalits remained landless even after allotment of land. This is clear from Table 1.2.

Table 1.2 : Dispossession of Land even after Allotment

Particular	*Number of Persons*	*Area in Hectares*
Total Entitlements given/Dispossessed	805146	81949587.00
Scheduled Castes	8775	9668.34
Scheduled Tribes	10896	15811.97
Other Backward Classes	5342	3793.12
Others	2240	3473.87
Total Disposed land	27253	32747.32

Source : Commissioners of Land Records and Settlements, M.P. Gwalior (upto December 1988).

Of the total land about 44.39 per cent was cultivable and 15.30 per cent was recorded as barren/waste land in the province of undivided M.P. The average landholding in the state was 2.6 hec. (Sharma, 2000:15). Only 12.6 per cent of the dalits in the state have lands, which constitute 8.1 per cent of the total landholding in the state. It is reported that 37.33 per cent of landholdings in the state are marginal holdings covering only 6.3 per cent of the total operated land, 22.82 per cent of land holdings are small holdings covering only 24.02 per cent of the area operated (NCAS and EP, 2002:16).

If we see the history of land reform in the M.P. from 1960 to 1992 we do not see any significant change despite claims made by political leaders and others. It is evident that 41.6 per cent of the landowners in the state have more than 100 acres of land although the land ceiling in rural areas is 18 acres of irrigated land (Sail 2002:60). The above pathetic state of affair continued towards the turn of the previous century. Even the effort taken by the Government of M.P. on March 4, 1998 through which it asked all the district Collectors to reduce the *Charnoi* land area from the existing 7.5 per cent of the total land mass reserved for grazing purposes to 5 per cent, the problem of landlessness was not solved among the weaker sections. During this phase 1.54 lakhs acres of land in the form of 80,470 *pattas* was, however, distributed to SC/ST families. This included 46,088 SC and 34,382 ST beneficiaries (*The Bhopal Document*, 2002, pp. 110-11) but in spite of it 16.22 per cent SC and 17.57 per cent ST were forced to remain landless and many more were landless. This is clear from Table 1.3.

Table 1.3 : Land Ownership Pattern among SC/ST in M.P.

Land in Acres	*Percentage of Land Ownership*		*Total Percent*
	Dalit	*Tribal*	
Landless	16.22	17.57	33.79
0.1-1.0	45.94	20.71	66.65
1.1-2.0	13.52	12.56	26.08
2.1-3.0	8.1	11.19	19.29
3.1-4.0	5.41	6.38	11.79
4.1-5.0	4.05	8.58	12.63
5.1-6.0	4.06	6.38	10.44
6+	12.70	16.63	19.33

Source: Land for Life, NCAS and Ekta Parished, Pune and Bhopal (2002), p. 32.

History and Status of *Charnoi* Land in M.P.

As stated earlier, under Section 234 of the M.P. Land Revenue Code, 1959 which came into practice from October 2, 1959 attempt was made to document the unoccupied land in the villages of M.P. Sections 234 of this Code deals with preparation of *Nistar Patrak* and how a *Nistar Patrak* is to be prepared, Sections 235 and 236 provide about the matters which will be included in the *Nistar Patrak*. Section 237 provides as under:

1. Subject to rules made under this Code, the Collector may set apart unoccupied land for the following purposes, namely:

(a) for timber or fuel reserve;

(b) for pasture, grass bir or fodder reserve;

(c) for burial ground and cremation ground;

(d) for gaothan;

(e) for encamping ground;

(f) for threshing floor;

(g) for bazar;

(h) for skinning ground;

(i) for manure pits;

(j) for public purposes such as schools, play grounds, park road, lanes, drains and the like; and

(k) for any other purposes which may be prescribed for the exercise of right of *Nistar*.

2. Lands set apart specially for any purpose mentioned in sub-section (1) shall not otherwise be diverted without the sanction of the Collector.

3. Subject to the rules made under this Code, the Collector may divert such unoccupied land, which is set apart for the purposes mentioned in clause (b) of sub-section (1). Subject to secure minimum 2 per cent of the agricultural land of that village for the said purposes into *abadi* or for agricultural purposes.

From 1959 till 1997 lands which were earmarked for *Charnoi* purpose (for grazing purpose) and how much will be that area and in what proportion with the cultivable area of the village was not governed by the Code but by the executive instructions. The executive instruction provided that if the village has 1000 acres of cultivable area then minimum 10 per cent area shall be kept reserved for *Charnoi* purpose (for grazing purpose), later on it was reduced to 7.5 per cent. With the experience it was felt that looking to the encroachments made on the grazing lands by the influential persons of the village it was thought that at least a provision is made that a minimum area of *Charnoi* land must remain in village and which cannot be either allotted or diverted. Keeping this object the State Legislature incorporated sub-section (3) in Section 237, wherein a provision has been made that minimum 5 per cent will have to be kept for *Nistar* purpose/*Charnoi* purpose. This amendment has been incorporated by M.P. Act No. 1 of 1998, which came into force on September 5, 1998. By second Amendment Act No. 23/2000, the area has been reduced from 5 per cent to 2 per cent. This amendment came into force on August 16, 2000.

In M.P. at the time when M.P. Land Revenue Code, 1959 came into force, the allotment of agricultural land to landless persons and other persons was governed by 162 of the Code which was deleted on April 13, 1964 by M.P. Act No. 25 of 1964 and it was replaced by executing instructions known as Revenue Book Circulars, popularly known as R.B.C. Part (IV-3) of R.B.C. contains the provision of allotment of agricultural lands to various categories of population. From time to time amendments have been made in the RBC. The Circular dated March 2, 2002 issued by the Government of M.P. which provides that the excess *Charnoi* land would be allotted to *Dalits* can be seen in the light of that amendment in RBC.

Bhopal Declaration: Ray of Hope for Dalits and Tribes

The distribution of *Charnoi* land under *Dalit Agenda* or *Bhopal Declaration* (2002) undertaken by Government of M.P. is a more serious and concerted effort with full of political will and social commitment to empower the poor dalits. Students of economic history in M.P. may have different views on why this effort was taken? How it is related to power struggle between the Congress and BJP? How and to what extent BSP has created political challenge for Congress in M.P.? Was there public demand in favour of distribution of *Charnoi* land among dalits and tribes? But it is beyond doubt that thousands of landless dalits amd tribes were made land owners within 47 days in 2002. This is a reality. And it is for the first time that such reality has been constructed by the

Government in M.P. With the allotment of more than 5 lakhs hec. of land among SC and ST in M.P. a new history has been created. It is needless to mention that the *Bhopal Declaration* popularly known as *Dalit Agenda* dated April 14, 2002 promised the poor dalits of (it inccluded ST also) M.P. to eliminate the problems of landlessness from among them. This declaration resolved 21 point-agenda for the empowerment of dalits and tribals. However, land to the landless fall under the first agenda. It states:

> "Ensure that each Dalit family will own enough cultivable land for socio-economic well-being. The government should pursue all possible measures including the distribution of surplus land, government revenue lands and temple lands within a specific timeframe. If the need be, the government should purchase cultivate land and distribute it among Dalits." (p.5)

Achievement

As per the government notification the scheme of distribution of grazing land began from April 14, 2002 and due to intervention of Jabalpur High Court it ended on the last day of May 2002. During this short period about 3,01,356 and 2,22,289 hec. of land were distributed among both categories of SC and ST families respectively. Here by category I, we mean landless households and category II refers to those households who possess upto 2.5 acres of poor quality land. District wise figure pertaining to distribution of land among both the categories of SC and ST households are presented below.

Table 1.4 : District-wise Distribution of *Charnoi* Land Among Categories-I and II Households Among SC/ST in Madhya Pradesh

District	*SC*			*ST*		
	Category I	*Category II*	*Total*	*Category I*	*Category II*	*Total*
Sheopur	1023	799	1822	2326	1764	4090
Morena	0	5213	5213	0	260	260
Bhind	770	2225	2995	0	0	0
Gwalior	0	2419	2419	0	1396	1396
Shivpuri	0	2267	2267	0	2047	2047

(Contd.)

Table 1.4 *(Contd.)*

Guna	0	1495	1495	0	2206	2206
Datia	923	1436	2359	393	302	695
Ujjain	4502	10792	15294	264	668	932
Dewas	2667	8596	11263	1785	6926	8711
Ratlam	0	0	0	0	1225	1225
Shajapur	242	264	506	51	239	290
Mandsaur	0	0	0	0	0	0
Neemuch	0	432	432	0	526	526
Indore	2779	2370	5149	467	2002	2469
Dhar	2487	4802	7289	4407	15109	19516
Jhabua	0	0	0	0	0	0
Khargoan	12939	2471	15410	10252	3057	13309
Barwani	1886	662	2548	3662	6620	10282
Khandawa	1535	305	1840	1679	337	2016
Bhopal	1805	530	2335	347	138	485
Sehore	1356	2896	4252	231	990	1221
Raisen	4055	4250	8305	3561	2301	5862
Rajgarh	0	1063	1063	226	323	549
Vidisha	3122	6332	9454	1047	1931	2978
Betul	1996	4207	6203	4557	12218	16775
Hosanga-bad	6244	101333	107577	4400	8803	13203
Harda	128	183	311	223	438	661
Sagar	2920	2793	5713	1765	1101	2866
Damoh	5135	4466	9601	2643	2436	5079
Panna	0	4781	4781	0	1481	1481
Chatarpur	1959	1596	3555	1000	1211	2211

(Contd.)

Table 1.4 *(Contd.)*

Tikamgarh	0	0	0	0	0	0
Jabalpur	4807	1502	6309	6900	2005	8905
Katani	2350	3481	5831	5523	6413	11936
Narsinghpur	1448	1107	2555	687	967	1654
Chhindwara	1507	2507	4014	2529	3985	6514
Seoni	2079	1792	3871	4132	5510	9642
Mandala	50	71	121	135	205	340
Dindori	29	319	348	740	2939	3679
Balaghat	3509	3366	6875	2592	3238	5830
Rewa	9897	9205	19102	14161	8698	22859
Shedole	836	1724	2560	4634	11317	15951
Satna	2036	3203	5239	1875	2854	4729
Umaria	0	0	0	0	138	138
Sidhi	985	2095	3080	2389	4382	6771
Total	**90006**	**211350**	**301356**	**91583**	**130706**	**222289**

Source: Obtained from the office of Secretary to the Chief Minister Dr. Amar Singh dated 21.8.2003.

Court Cases and State Response

In reaction to this step from different parts of the state about 55 writ petitions were filed in the High Court of Jabalpur. The complaints mostly those who had already encroached the *Charnoi* land long back pleaded before the High Court to declare the decision of Government of M.P. dated 2.3.2002 null and void and also requested for withdrawal of the allotted land from the allottees. They provided many arguments to support their demand. Few important among these are the following:

1. It was submitted by the petitioners that they are poor. They were cultivating certain Gochar lands since long. They filed Khasras to show their possession. Some said that their

application for allotment of land is pending. They lamented that no effort can be made legally to evict them from possession without deciding their pending case. Many of them also requested that legally *Charnoi* lands cannot be allotted to anybody and if it has to be allotted, it may be allotted to them only because already they are cultivating these lands. They have made it useful after constant investment.

2. Some petitioners said that since they are also poor like SC and ST population, therefore, it should be only allotted to them. To them action of the government pertaining to allotment of land only to the SC/ST persons is illegal, contrary to law and violative of Articles 14 and 15 of the Constitution of India. Monopoly cannot be created in favour of SC and ST persons. Benefit of 100 per cent reservation cannot be extended to them. This is the violation of right of equality of opportunity.

3. Some petitioners said that land used by them cannot be treated as "unoccupied" land. It should be treated as occupied land. Hence, it should not be snatched away from one landless section for another landless people. If it is snatched they will be made to starve.

4. Some petitioners said that *Charnoi* land cannot be converted into agricultural land and thereby they have planted only fruit bearing trees on these lands. To them deduction of *Charnoi* land from 5 per cent to 2 per cent is against the provisions of the *Adhiniyam* of 1984 and the concerned Code. Under Section 239 of the Code the petitioners are, therefore, entitled for the use of fruits of trees.

5. In W.P. No. 2730/2002 a plea was taken that Collector is not empowered to convert *gocher* land into agricultural land without following the procedure prescribed under the Code. Therefore, the total process of allotment of *Charnoi* land to SC and ST population for agricultural purpose is illegal and uncalled for.

6. Some petitioners demanded that *"Khalihan"* and land reserved for other purposes under Section 237 of the Code cannot be used/allotted for the purpose of cultivation.

Respondent's Reaction

The Government of M.P. made its attempt through the Advocate General in the High Court to defend its decision and action pertaining to allotment of land. The main arguments were the following:

1. The petitioners after illegally occupying the grazing land have developed it and made it cultivable at their own. This is totally illegal and uncalled for. On the basis of its illegal possession they cannot be made its owners no matter since when they are cultivating. They are actually encroachers and on this unlawful basis land cannot be allotted to them. Under Section 237 of the Code and under Section 3 of the *M.P. Krishi Prayojan Ke Liye Upayog ki Ja Rahi Dakhal Rahit Bhoomi Par Bhoomiswami Adhikaron ka Pradan Kiya Jana Adhiniyam* (1984) the illegal possessors are not entitled for this land. Since SC/ST people are oppressed most therefore such lands have been allotted to them only.

2. The respondents said that in the past Collector was empowered to allot such lands under Section 162 of the Code. Today allotment as per the executive instructions contained in Annexure R1, R2, R3, R4, R5 and R6 (issued on 2nd March 2002) Revenue Inspector is empowered to deal with such lands. This charge has been made to fulfil the constitutional obligation infavour of the SC/ST population and to ensure their welfare. This action is legal because it has been taken in accordance with the provisions of Sections 233 and 237.

High Court Decision

Besides the above two main legal/technical arguments many other arguments were also provided by the Advocate General infavour of the government decision. However, the High Court made its decision infavour of the petitioners. It said:

> "Resultantly, the circular dated 2.3.2002 (R6) is quashed and consequently the circular dated 19.9.2000 and the circulars R1 to R5 which have merged in final modified circular dated 2.3.2002, falls down and the action taken pursuant thereto is illegal and void, the respondents are restrained from converting

the land and directed to preserve the land for the public purpose for which it has been reserved and to use the land for the purpose it has been reserved under Section 237 of the Code. Respondents are restrained from converting the land reserved under Section 237 and to allot it to any persons on the basis of said circulars. It is further directed that such lands which have been reserved under Section 237 be freed from encroachment expeditiously. Costs on parties" *(Annexure- P-1: Copy of the order dated 5.8.2002 passed by the High Court of M.P. Jabalpur in W.P. No. 2496/2002).*

That the Petitioners submitted letters Patent Appeal before the High Court and by the impugned order the High Court set aside the order dated 5.8.2002 passed by the learned single judge but also issued directions which were made by the High Court in its judgment dated 16.1.2003 in W.P. No. 6973/2002, marked Annexure P-2 and connected matters wherein it was directed that the State Government shall prepare the scheme for allotment of land and SC and ST persons will not be given any priority on the basis of the caste and the State Government will not distribute any further land from the excess *Charnoi* area and the State Government has been further directed to arrange the land apart from the lands set apart under Section 237(1) and match the same by way of matching land allotment to equalize with 50 per cent. The same directions have been reiterated in the impugned order dated 16.1.2003 also.

Therefore, to the extent directions have been made by the High Court for not giving priority of allotment of land to SC and ST communities this Special Leave Petition is filed against the impugned order. A separate special leave petition has also been filed against the Order dated 16.1.2003 passed in Writ Petition W.P. No. 6973/2002 and connected matters.

Against the above order dated 16.1.2003 of High Court, Jabalpur, the Government of M.P. filed Special Leave Petition in the Supreme Court of India, New Delhi dated 30.6.2003. Till then the process of distribution of land is discontinued.

But this is the legal and procedural dimension of the phenomenon. SC and ST beneficiaries in large number have already receied grazing land under this scheme. How and to what extent they have perceived this development? How access to and control over land have impacted them psychologically, socially, economically and politically? What is the sustainability of their rosy experience? These are some of the broad issues which have been covered in all the three papers included in this volume. When all the three studies, on which these three articles included in this volume are based, were conducted, M.P. had 45 districts and the study was conducted in 20 districts. These 20 districts represent the entire length and breath of the state. Hence, conclusion drawn by these studies may also be applicable for the entire state.

References

Kurukeshtra, (1986): October issue, pp. 59-63.

Lal Bahadur Shastri Academy of Administration (1994): " A Report on Land Reforms in Madhya Pradesh : An Empirical Study (1988-1991)" *Land Reforms in India: Issues of Equality in Rural M.P.* (ed) P.K. Jha, Vol. 7, New Delhi: Sage.

Mainstream, May 6, 1972:17.

Mainstream (1972) : Madhya Pradesh : Ceilings, Exemptions and Loopholes, May 6, 17-19.

NCAS and Ekta Parishad (2002) : *Land for Life: Promise and Performance of Land Reforms in Madhya Pradesh,* Pune.

R.A. Gautam and K. Prasad (2001) : *Madhya Pradesh Ke Dalit,* New Delhi: Indian Social Institute.

Sail, K.R. (2002) : "People's Struggle for Land–A Case Study" in *Land Reforms in India: Issues of Equity in Rural Madhya Pradesh* (ed.) P.K. Jha, Vol. 7, New Delhi: Sage.

Sankaran, R. (1996) : "Introduction" in *Land Reform in India,* (ed.) B.N. Yugandhar, Vol. 3, New Delhi : Sage.

Sharma, R. (2000), Unheard Voice : A Research Report (unpublished) on land distribution from Vidisha district of M.P., Bhopal. *The Bhopal Document* (2002), Government of M.P., Bhopal.

The Task Force Report on Bhopal Declaration (2003), Government of M.P. Bhopal, p. 5.

2

Grazing Land to Dalits in Sehore : Case Study

— *S.N. Chaudhary*

The paper intends to examine process of allotment of a portion of grazing land among dalits of Sehore villages and its implications. It is divided into eight parts. The opening part deals with the socio-physical context where the study was conducted. In the second part social profile of the beneficiaries have been described. Third part deals with process and steps involved in land allotment. In the fourth part status and features of the allotted land have been documented. It also deals with some of the consequences of land allotment. Fifth part deals with land use pattern and its socio-economic and psychological impact on beneficiaries. In part sixth attempt has been made to map perceptions of "others" about the total land allotment process and its consequences. Under part seventh case studies of five beneficiaries have been presented. Towards the end concluding observations have been made.

I

Socio-Physical Context

The study was conducted in 13 villages of Sehore Development Block (SDB) falling under Sehore district. Sehore district headquarter located at Sehore town is situated at a distance of about 39 kms. from Bhopal. There are five *tehsils* in the district of which Sehore is one. As per 1991 Census the population size of the district is 10,78,769 of which 20.30 per cent consists of the dalit population. *Dhobi, Nai, Balai* and *Chamar* are the major dalit castes. The district is underdeveloped in terms of literacy rate, per capita income, size of landholding, sex-ratio, facility of toilet and drinking water and so on. Further, in spite of recent intervention by the State through Education Gurantee Scheme (EGS) and *Padhna Badna Andolan* and transfer of local level educational activities to the *Gram Panchayat* the problem of drop-out among the girl students and the problem of untouchability and alcoholism particularly among the dalit population in very high.

So far as, SDB is concerned, there are 127 *Gram Panchayats* with having 301 villages. 13 multi-caste villages were identified to conduct the proposed study. It is needless to mention that out of 301 villages *Charnoi* land was distributed in 209 villages. However, in large number of villages (146) less than 20 dalit families received land under the scheme. This is clear from Table 2.1.

Table 2.1: Distribution of *Charnoi* Land in the Villages of Sehore Development Block (SDB)

	Number of Villages/ Households	*Number of Sampled Villages/ Households*
Number of Villages in SDB	301	13
Number of Villages in SDB where *Charnoi* land was distributed	209	13
Villages where more than 50 households were allotted land	6	No
Villages where between 40-50 households were allotted land	3	No
Villages where between 30-40 beneficiaries were allotted land	19	1
Villages where between 20-30 households were allotted land	35	3
Villages where less than 20 households were allotted land	146	9
Number of beneficiaries household in all 209 villages	3460	200

Source : Office of S.D.M., Sehore dated 19.8.2003.

Sampling

We identified 13 villages for the purpose of the study. After obtaining relevant data from the district headquarter and conducting baseline survey by using interview Schedule-I in 13 villages we came to know that among 232 dalit households *Charnoi* land was distributed. Since the number of beneficiaries household was not very big, therefore, we decided to conduct study on all these 232 households.

Table 2.2 : Villagewise Number of Households/Dalit Households and the Sampled Households which Participated in the Study

Sl. No.	*Village Name*	*Total HHs*	*SC HHs*	*SC/ST HHs Allowed Land*	*Total land alloted in Village (n hec.)*	*Sampled HHs*	*HHs Possessng Land*	*HHs who's lands are Possessed by "others"*	*Cast Background of "Others"*				
									Mewara	*Balai*	*Khari*	*Parmar*	*Pawar*
(1)	(2)	(3)	(4)	(5)	(6)	(7)	(8)	(9)	(10)	(11)	(12)	(13)	(14)
1.	Thunakhurd	88	27	23	41.863	21	21	02	1	1	-	-	-
2.	Mographool	124	50	14	24.497	02	13	01	-	-	1	-	-
3.	Sonda	127	47	9	5.679	09	09	-	-	-	-	-	-
4.	Alampura	90	10	18	14.515	02	09	01	-	-	-	1	-
5.	Panch Pipaliya	116	40	24	14.180	24	24	-	-	-	-	-	-
6.	Mungwali	126	41	16	22.013	16	16	-	-	-	-	-	-
7.	Kharpa	75	41	21	11.474	16	16	05	-	-	-	-	5
8.	Chapri	83	29	10	16.646	10	10	-	-	-	-	-	-
9.	Chitodia Van	103	61	31	26.058	31	31	-	-	-	-	-	-
10.	Pipaliya Meera	106	27	15	11.289	12	12	03	3	-	-	-	-
11.	Londiya	86	21	20	27.275	19	19	01	-	-	1	-	-
12.	Chitodia Lakha	85	30	22	17.398	22	22	-	-	-	-	-	-
13.	Amla	84	27	17	14.252	16	17	-	-	-	-	-	-
	Total	1294	451	240	247.139	200	219	13	4	1	2	1	5

Sources: 1. For column (2), (3), (4), (5), (5), (6), (7), (8), (9), (10) field data.

2. For column (6) information obtained from S.D.M. office, Sehore dated 29.9.2003.

But during the time of study only 213 head of the households were available for this study. Further, in course of study we came to know that all the 213 households had no possession of the allotted land. Actually 13 households have received allotment paper but till date even after several months of allotment land is not under their possession. The land allotted to them are still under the illegal possession of the village influential. We collected details from all these 13 households but our intensive study was conducted only on 200 households. The villagewise number of the households which participated in the study are presented in Table 2.2.

Research Questions

The study was conducted with the following specific research questions:

1. Whether lands have been distributed to the real eligible categories?
2. Whether the beneficiaries are in the physical possession of land?
3. Whether *pattas* and other relevant papers have been issued to the beneficiaries?
4. Whether the distributed land is problematic in terms of its distance from home, location on the hill, encroachment by somebody, forest/disputed land and its uncultivable nature?
5. Whether any agricultural inputs such as irrigation, seeds, fertilizers, cash, cultivation cost were also provided to the beneficiaries along with land?
6. Whether the beneficiaries are utilizing the land for agriculture or lying unused?
7. Whether the allotted land is economically viable?
8. How possession/use of land have affected the beneficiaries socially, economically and politically?
9. Whether the allottees have stopped seasonal migration as a result of allotment of land?
10. What is the reaction of the other castes or community who did not receive land?
11. Has the distribution of land resulted in any conflict, caste, class or otherwise?

12. Are there still *Charnoi* land/wasteland available for distribution in the village?
13. Are there still landless people available in the village?
14. How the amount of benefit of *Charnoi* land may be increased and ensured?

Features of Thirteen Villages

Availability of Infrastructure in the Sampled Villages

All the 13 villages are similar to each other in different ways. For instance, all the villages have the facility of temple, school, *anganwadi bhawan*, public and private well and public hand pump. But only 2 villages have the facility of PDS and health centre. Similarly, only few villages have the facility of post office, play ground and common means of entertainment. One village has the facility of common toilet. Since majority of respondents do not have sufficient amount of food for them for the entire year. Therefore, less number of PDS and that also in only two villages is unfortunate. Similarly, the less number of health centre and common toilet as well as no private toilet facility at all show that health is not seriously perceived in the villages. The common facility available in the villages are water, school, anganwadi centres, private shops and temple. On an average for each of the two villages there are 3 temples. But it is reported that dalits have neither access to nor control over these temples. In many cases they are forcefully denied when they make effort for temple entry. Unavailability or near absence of river, tank and forest in most of the villages do not allow dalits to depend upon common resources for their livelihood. Similarly, lack of metalled road restrict their mobility particularly in the rainy season. Availability of common facilities are evident from Table 2.3.

Social Organizations/Problems

Near absence of NGO, Self-Help Group and Mahila Mandali do not ensure formation of social capital in more than 75 per cent villages. Here by social capital we mean "The set of resources that inhere in family relations, trust, norms and networks that can improve the efficiency of society by facilitating coordinated actions" (Putnam, 1993). Hans Blomkvist and Ashok Swain (2001) also

Table 2.3 : Availability of Infrastructure in the Sampled Villages

Village Name	Items																				
	Public Well	*Private Well*	*Public Hand Pump*	*Private Hand Pump*	*River*	*Tank*	*Forest*	*Metalled Road*	*Mohallah*	*Panchayat/Public*	*School*	*Aganwadi Bhawan*	*Health Centre*	*PDS*	*Shop*	*Play Ground*	*Means of*	*Temple*	*Mosque*	*Post Office*	*Common Toilet*
(1)	(2)	(3)	(4)	(5)	(6)	(7)	(8)	(9)	(10)	(11)	(12)	(13)	(14)	(15)	(16)	(17)	(18)	(19)	(20)	(21)	(22)
Chitodia Van	2	125	4	3	-	-	-	-	2	-	1	1	-	-	3	-	1	3	-	-	-
Chitodia Lakha	4	3	4	-	-	-	-	-	5	-	1	1	-	-	-	-	-	1	-	-	-
Panch Pipaliya	5	120	3	-	-	-	-	-	4	1	3	1	-	-	3	-	1	1	-	1	-
Aamla	1	50	7	-	-	-	-	-	4	-	1	-	-	-	-	1	1	3	-	-	-
Mongra Phool	4	100	7	1	-	-	-	-	3	1	1	1	-	-	4	-	1	2	1	-	-
Pipariya Meera	-	-	10	1	-	1	1	-	4	1	-	1	1	-	5	1	1	1	-	-	-
Londiya	1	100	5	-	-	-	-	-	2	1	1	1	-	-	2	1	-	2	-	-	1
Sonda	1	24	8	1	1	-	1	1	4	1	1	1	-	1	5	1	1	1	-	-	-
Chapri	1	3	6	2	1	-	1	1	4	-	1	1	-	-	3	-	-	1	1	-	-
Mungawali	-	30	13	30	1	1	-	1	4	-	4	1	1	1	5	-	1	3	-	1	-
Alampura	1	8	8	35	-	1	-	-	3	-	1	-	-	-	-	1	1	2	-	-	-
Thunakhurd	1	45	4	4	-	1	-	-	2	-	1	1	-	-	2	-	-	1	-	-	-
Kharpa	1	30	2	-	1	-	1	-	2	1	2	1	-	-	-	-	1	1	-	-	-
Total	**22**	**638**	**81**	**77**	**4**	**4**	**4**	**3**	**43**	**6**	**18**	**11**	**2**	**2**	**32**	**5**	**9**	**22**	**2**	**2**	**1**

said that "Social capital refers to trusts, networks and norms shared by a group of actors that enables them to act together more effectively to pursue shared objectives" (p. 638).

In some of the villages there is presence of political parties and in these villages only, one can see the presence of large number of factions. In other words, in all the 6 villages where political parties are in existence, there are about 20 factions. These factions are on both caste and political party line. It is needless to mention that irrespective of their caste background majority of the villagers are the supporter of Congress party. On an average 3 factions are available in each of these 6 villages. At the same time cases of untouchability, number of litigation and number of government run development projects are available in all the villages. Only 2 villages have dalits organization, but in these villages also like other villages minimum wage rate is not followed. We could locate the practice of child labour in only 3 villages. The number of handicapped person is very high (89) and it is available in all the villages, but there are hardly any social organization to deal with their problem. There is nothing like local market in the area and majority of the villages of Sehore Development Block depend on Sehore town for their day-to-day requirement. Only in 3 villages few people subscribe newspaper. There are caste panchayat in 5 villages and in most of these villages we see the presence of political parties and social factions. This is clear from Table 2.4.

Social and Demographic Profile

There are 1294 households with having 7655 population in all the 13 villages where the study was conducted. Hence, on an average there are 92 households and 589 population in each of the villages. Majority of the houses (59%) are *kaccha* but at the same time 82 per cent of the total houses are constructed on the private ancestral land although 17 per cent houses are located on community/ government land. The finding reveals that male outnumber the female population, children outnumber the population from above 30 years and as we move up from 20 years of age in the age hierarchy, the number of population in different age groups significantly decreases. The number of married and unmarried is the same and the number of widow/widower is only 3 per cent.

Table 2.4 : Social Organizations/Problems

Village Name	*NGO*	*Self-Help Group*	*Function*	*Mahila Mandli*	*Polititical Party*	*Case of Untouchability since last 5 Years*	*Case of Dowry in last 5 Years*	*Number of Handicapped*	*Government Run Development Schemes*	*Courts Cases*	*Dalit Organizatoin*	*Wage Rate*			*Local Market*	*Public Transport*	*Newspaper*	*Caste Panchayat*
												F	M	C				
(1)	(2)	(3)	(4)	(5)	(6)	(7)	(8)	(9)	(10)	(11)	(12)	(13)	(14)	(15)	(16)	(17)	(18)	(19)
Chitodia Van	-	-	-	-	-	Yes	-	6	Yes	Yes	-	30	40	-	-	-	-	-
Chitodia Lakha	Yes	-	-	-	-	Yes	-	4	Yes	Yes	-	25	30	-	-	-	-	-
Panch Pipaliya	-	-	-	-	-	Yes	-	10	Yes	Yes	-	25	30	-	-	-	-	-
Aamla	-	-	-	-	-	Yes	-	4	Yes	Yes	-	25	30	-	-	Yes	-	-
Mongra Phool	-	-	-	-	-	Yes	-	5	Yes	Yes	-	25	25	-	-	-	-	Yes
Pipariya Meera	-	-	-	-	-	Yes	Yes	8	Yes	Yes	Yes	25	30	-	-	-	-	-
Londiya	-	-	4	-	Yes	Yes	-	4	Yes	Yes	Yes	20	25	-	-	Yes	Yes	-
Sonda	Yes	-	3	1	Yes	-	-	10	Yes	Yes	-	25	25	-	-	Yes	Yes	-
Chapri	-	-	3	2	Yes	Yes	-	5	Yes	Yes	-	30	30	25	-	Yes	-	Yes
Mungawali	-	2	4	-	Yes	Yes	-	20	Yes	Yes	-	25	25	25	-	Yes	Yes	Yes
Alampura	-	1	4	-	Yes	Yes	-	3	Yes	Yes	-	25	30	-	-	Yes	-	Yes
Thunakhurd	1	-	-	-	Yes	-	8	Yes	Yes	-	30	30	20	-	-	-	Yes	
Kharpa	-	-	2	-	Yes	Yes	-	2	Yes	Yes	-	25	25	-	-	-	-	-
		4	20	3				89										

Note: "Yes" only refer to the availability and not the nunber.

Table 2.5 : Socio-Economic Profile of Villagers

Sex	*Male*	*Female*	*Total*
Freq.	4178	3477	7655
%	55	45	100

Age	*0-9*	*10-19*	*20-29*	*30-39*	*40-49*	*50-59*	*60+*	*Total*
Freq.	1538	1538	1518	990	667	399	368	7655
%	20	20	20	13	9	5	5	100

Marital Status	*Not Applicable*	*Unmarried*	*Married*	*Widow/Widower*	*Total*
Freq.	2747	960	3752	197	7655
%	36	13	49	3	100

Occupation	*N.A.*	*Cast Occupation*	*Labour*	*Agriculture +*	*Agriculture Labour*	*Private Job*	*Business*	*Government Job*	*Artisan*	*Husbandry Work*	*Other*	*Total*
Freq.	4211	57	84	1233	1164	44	37	23	13	17	10	7655
%	55	1	11	16	15	1	0	0	0	0	0	100

(Contd.)

Table 2.5 *(Contd.)*

Education	*N.A.*	*Illiterate*	*Literate*	*Primary*	*Middle*	*High School*	*Higher Secondary*	*U.G/P.G*	*Professional*	*Total*
Freq.	1571	3230	148	1416	766	356	102	67	1	7655
%	21	42	2	18	10	5	1	1	0	100

Annual Income	*Nothing*	*Upto Rs. 5000*	*5000-10000*	*10000-15000*	*15000-20000*	*20000-25000*	*25000+*	*Total*
Freq.	4256	675	1283	919	297	105	120	7655
%	56	9	17	12	4	1	2	100

Land Ownership (H.H.)	*Landless*	*Upto 2.5 acress*	*2.5 acres +*	*Total H.Hs.*
Freq.	250	337	707	1294
%	19	26	55	100

Maximum number of people are dependent population (55%). Actually they are children, women and the aged, but maximum number of those engaged in income work are engaged in labour, agriculture and both (42%) work. Business and job is a rare phenomena. Further, majority of the population (63%) is either minor or illiterate. The number of population with higher and technical education is hardly one per cent. While majority of population (56%) have no income there are about 2 per cent, i.e. 120 persons who have income of either/or more than Rs. 25000 per annum. But the number of landless is much lower (19%) in comparison to those households which (55%) possess more than 2.5 acres of land. However, this refers to the current situation, particularly majority of dalit households have already possessed the allotted land. This is clear from Table 2.5.

Caste Background

Of the total 1294 households in all the 13 villages the OBC outnumber the population of other castes or caste groups. This is because they constitute 53.63 per cent of population. The general category population constitute only 3.32 per cent. So far as SC are concerned they constitute second largest population (35.55%) in the villages. However, among them *Chamar* and *Balai* are numerically dominant. This is because while former constitute about 18 per cent of the total population the later constitute about 14 per cent of the entire population. We could identify only 5 ST HHs in the villages but Muslims constitute about 7.11 per cent of population. This is clear from Table 2.5.

Table 2.6 : Caste Background of Households in 13 Villages

Caste	*General*	*OBC*	*SC*						*ST*	*Muslims*	*Total*
			Total	*Chamar*	*Balai*	*Selawat*	*Sapera*	*Mehtar*			
Fre.	43	694	460	232	179	35	9	5	5	92	1294
%	3.32	53.63	35.55	17.93	13.83	2.70	0.70	0.39	0.39	7.11	100

Household Assets

All the households in thirteen villages are by and large electrified. As a result, the number of households with having facility of television, radio and tape recorder, fan and cooler etc., is high i.e. 53, 42 and 67 per cent respectively. But telephone connection is available in hardly one per cent of households. Grain storage facility is available in 35 per cent of households. But facility of latrine, tap water, newspaper etc., is available with only limited or insignificant number of households. Availability of television set in large number of households and availability of toilet and newspaper facility in very small number of households clearly reflect the impact of consumer culture in backward villages of Sehore district. This is clear from Table 2.7.

Table 2.7 : Household Assets/Facility

Items	*Total*	*Yes*	*%*	*No*	*%*
Electricity	1294	1276	99	18	1
Telephone	1294	7	1	1287	99
Television	1294	686	53	608	47
Radio/Tape recorder	1294	541	42	753	58
Two Wheeler	1294	289	22	1005	78
Latrine	1294	75	6	1219	94
Sewing Machine	1294	175	14	1119	86
Bank/Post Office Account	1294	493	38	801	62
Grain Storage	1294	455	35	839	65
Cooler/Fan	1294	866	67	428	33
Refrigerator	1294	16	1	1278	99
Four Wheeler	1294	15	1	1279	99
Tap Water	1294	60	5	1234	95
Newspaper	1294	21	2	1273	98
Food for whole year	1294	521	40	773	60
Drawing room	1294	235	18	1059	82

Agricultural Assets

Of course, there is modernization in agriculture but both traditional and modern technological instruments are available in the sampled villages. Availability of tractor, thresher, sprayer, tube well, ox/plough and bullock cart in 7,10, 8, 24, 29 and 28 per cent households prove this fact. At the same time as we move from traditional to modern and within modern relatively familiar to relatively less familiar technology, its number decreases. Availability of ox/plough in 29 per cent households and availability of tractor in only 7 per cent households prove this fact. Domestication of milch cattle is very common in the sampled villages. It is available with 73 per cent households. This is obvious from Table 2.8.

Table 2.8 : Agricultural Assets and Cattle

Items	*Total*	*Yes*	*%*	*No*	*%*
Tractor	1294	91	7	1203	93
Thresher	1294	124	10	1170	90
Sprayer	1294	101	8	1193	92
Cow/Buffalo	1294	944	73	349	27
Goat	1294	153	12	1141	88
Tube-well	1294	313	24	981	76
Ox/Plough	1294	380	29	914	71
Bullock cart	1294	363	28	931	72

Saving/Indebtedness among Dalit Households

There are 461 dalit households in all the 13 villages. Majority of them (372) are under debt. Most of them have taken loan of either/ or more than Rs. 5000. The main source of loan is informal (villagers). Only limited number of the dalits have taken loan from the cooperative bank or formal institution. People also take loan from the local shopkeeper and *sahukar*. And the main purpose behind loan is to meet contingent/social expenditure. Few of them (43) have taken loan for agricultural purpose. In other words, of the total loanees 211 took loan for feeding purpose only. Only 2 Dalit households said that they had saving.

Land Distribution

Out of 461 dalit households 232 received land under *Bhopal Declaration* distributed by the Government during last two years.

Most of these households are from below the poverty line. But majority of them (170) received land upto 2.5 acres only. This is clear from Table 2.9.

Table 2.9 : Distribution of Land in Acres

Response	*Frequency*	*%*
Upto 2.5 acres	170	73.27
2.5 to 3.5 acres	28	12.06
Above 3.5 acres	25	10.77
Do not know	09	03.87
Total	**232**	**100**

Instrument

Besides depending on the conventional sources of data collection like secondary source we used four interview schedule, to collect information from different corners. For instance, interview Schedule I was used to know about demography and family owned infrastructure of all the households of 13 villages. On this basis we could know caste/class profile of each of the households in the villages. This information helped us to know number of the beneficiary households. Interview Schedule II was administered on the sampled dalit households. It was by and large administered on head of the households. This Schedule contained questions pertaining to socio-economic consequences of the distribution of *Charnoi* land on beneficiary households in particular and the local society in general and other issues. It was administered on 200 beneficiary households living in the villages of Sehore Development Block. Interview Schedule III was used on cross- section of local level population both dalit and non-dalit, government officials and panchayat representatives. Purpose of use of this Schedule was to comprehend the perception of "others" regarding distribution of *Charnoi* land and its overall implications. Interview Schedule IV was administered on Panchayat Secretary/Sarpanch, relatively rich dalit and non-dalit villagers and so on to know about infrastructural facilities, natural resources and major social practices in the villages.

II

Who are Beneficiaries ?

Attitude and behaviour is governed by variety of factors. One among these is the environment. Extreme social environmentalist and the western sociologists representing sociologistic school of thought including internationally known expert on sociology of knowledge Karl Manheim said that our attitude, likings and dislikings, feeling, observation, behaviour and action are determined by social environment. In Indian context when we examine attitude, behaviour and experience of either individual or group of individuals particularly living in the rural areas we cannot understand them without understanding their social background and social context where they live. Social background includes both ascribed and achieved social profile. Within the ascribed social profile we include birth based indicators such as age, sex, marital status, caste and religious background. In the case of achieved background we include those indices which are flexible and attend on the basis of efforts. Understanding of both these set of background variables is essential to understand the respondents, their behaviour and experience in totality.

Birth Based Indices

Age and Sex

There are 1029 members in all our 200 households where the study was conducted. Hence, on an average there are 5 members in each of the households. Similarly the number of children and grownup children upto the age of 19 years is much larger, i.e. about 50 per cent of the total members and as we moved towards upper age group right from 20 years onwards, the number of family members decreased from 21 to 4 per cent. In other words, while the number of children between the age group of 0-9 years is 294 (29%) the number of senior citizens who are above the age of 60 years is only 38 (4%). Hence, roughly speaking 4 per cent population in sampled households are the senior citizens.

So far as sex background is concerned, like the national and the state level trend in Madhya Pradesh in this case also male population significantly outnumbered the female population. In other words, 55 per cent members are men and the remaining 45 per cent are women.

Marital Status

As the number of children is much higher, therefore, 36 per cent of the total members are not even upto the age of their marriage. Twelve per cent members are unmarried. But 49 per cent are married. This shows the universality of marriage among the sampled households in particular and the villages under study in general. The number of widow/widower is only 3 per cent.

Caste

Although only the scheduled caste respondents participated in the study but interms of their sub-caste background they are different to each other. All the 200 respondents are from different sub-castes but *Sapera, Selawat* and *Mehtar* costitute hardly 15 per cent of their number. Majority of the respondents, i.e. 45 per cent and 42 per cent are from *Chamar* and *Balai* sub-caste respectively. This is clear from Table 2.10.

Table 2.10 : Sub-caste Background of Respondents

Sl.No.	*Sub-castes*	*Frequency*	*%*
1	Chamar	89	45
2	Balai	84	42
3	Mehtar	1	1
4	Selawat	21	11
5	Sapera	5	3
	Total	**200**	**100**

Achieved Background

Occupation

Majority of the respondents and their family members are either labour, marginal farmers and both and the dependent population. Mainly it is the children and women who are the dependent population. Only 3 per cent family members are mainly engaged in agricultural activities. Similarly hardly about 10 members are engaged in caste occupation, government and private jobs and other activities. Hence, the respondents and their family members are not associated with secondary and tertiary occupation. They (earning hands) are only engaged in the primary sector.

Annual Income

Since their main source of livelihood revolve around agriculture and technological modernization in agriculture is not very enthusiastic and developed, therefore, the level of their annual income is also very low. In other words, out of total 1029 members 532 are dependent population, 141 earn either/or less than Rs. 5000 per annum, 294 earn between Rs. 5000 to 10000 per annum and only 62, i.e. 6 per cent members earn either/or more than Rs. 10000 per annum. Hence, if on the basis of only their annual income we measure their poverty level, we can safely say that by and large the households under study are from below the poverty line. This is clear from Table 2.11.

Land Holding

Generally it is perceived that majority of the dalit households in the villages are related to land not as a owner but as a wage-earner. This means majority of them are either landless or they possess meagre amount of land, which is unable to meet their food requirement. But in this case the situation is slightly different. This is because 19 per cent households have no knowledge but 28 per cent households possess more than 2.5 acres of land. At the same time 53 per cent possess land but it is only upto 2.5 acres. In other words, in this study it is clear that 81 per cent households have land and only 19 per cent have no knowledge about the exact amount of land possessed by them. However, before allotment of land under the above agenda most of them were landless.

House

Sixty per cent respondents have constructed their houses on their own lands. But the remaining 13, 6 and 21 per cent have constructed it on the government land, village land and the community land respectively. If we combine community land and government land together it is clear that 34 per cent respondents have constructed their houses on government land. It is needless to mention that 86 per cent houses are *kaccha* and the remaining 14 per cent mixed. However, none of the houses are *pucca*.

Education

The level of literacy and education among the respondents and their family member is pitiable. While 21 per cent are minor children, therefore, they cannot go to school but 49 per cent of the total members, i.e. 500 are illiterate. The number of literate and educated upto high school level is however 31 per cent. We could hardly trace 5 members from the entire 200 households who had education upto higher secondary and college level. On this basis it is clear that the level of education is very poor among the respondents and their family members. Therefore, the schemes directed to promote education have still to show its visible presence.

Indebtedness and Saving

Since majority of the households are poor, majority of its members are illiterate and for livelihood majority of them are engaged in agricultural work either as labour or possess small amount of land, therefore, majority of them (169) are under debt. Majority of them (72%) have taken loan between Rs. 1000 to Rs. 5000. Since they live in villages, therefore, majority of them, i.e. 60 per cent have taken loan from villagers and relatives, and 15 per cent have taken loan from the local shopkeeper. At the same time 10 per cent have taken loan from local bank/ cooperatives.

Since the source of loan is informal, therefore, 84 per cent have taken loan to meet social expenditure, i.e. for feeding, marriage, treatment and so on. Only 11 per cent households have taken loan for agricultural purpose. Since about 85 per cent households are under debt, therefore, the number of households having saving is not available. Few of them are of course not under debt but at the same time they do not have saving at all.

Household Assets

Since majority of the households are poor with having less amount of income and education and majority of them are under debt, therefore, the level of availability of household assets particularly the modern one is very low. It is needless to mention that 98 per cent households have electricity connection. As a result, 31 and

Table 2.11 : Socio-economic profile of respondents and family members

Sex	*Male*	*Female*	*Total*
Freq.	562	467	1029
%	55	45	100

Age	*0-9*	*10-19*	*20-29*	*30-39*	*40-49*	*50-59*	*60+*	*Total*
Freq.	294	204	121	138	92	51	38	1029
%	19	20	21	13	9	5	4	100

Marital Status	*Not Applicable*	*Unmarried*	*Married*	*Widow/Widower*	*Total*
Freq.	2746	960	3752	197	7655
%	36	13	49	3	100

Occupation	*N.A.*	*Cast Occupation*	*Labour*	*Agriculture +*	*Agriculture Labour*	*Private Job*	*Business*	*Government Job*	*Artisan*	*Husbandry Work*	*Other*	*Total*
Freq.	525	4	275	35	183	2	-	1	-	-	4	1029
%	51	-	27	3	18	-	-	-	-	-	-	100

(Contd.)

Table 2.11 *(Contd.)*

Education	*N.A.*	*Illiterate*	*Literat e*	*Primary*	*Middle*	*High School*	*Higher Secondary*	*U.G/P.G*	*Professional*	*Total*
Freq.	212	500	33	182	39	28	2	3	-	1029
%	21	49	3	18	7	3	-	-	-	100

Annual Income	*Nothing*	*Upto Rs. 5000*	*5000-10000*	*10000-15000*	*15000-20000*	*20000-25000*	*25000+*	*Total*
Freq.	532	141	294	62	-	-	-	1029
%	52	14	29	6	-	-	-	100

Land Ownership (H.H.)	*No Knowledge*	*Upto 2.5 acres*	*2.5 acres +*	*Total H.Hs.*
Freq.	38	106	56	200
%	19	63	28	100

House on whose land	*Government*	*Viillagers*	*Community*	*Self*	*Total*
Freq.	26	12	42	120	200
%	13	06	21	60	100

Structure of House	*Kaccha*	*Mixed*	*Total*
Freq.	172	28	200
%	86	14	100

43 per cent households have the facility of television as well as radio/tape recorder respectively. Since government run development projects are working in villages, therefore, 24 per cent of them have their accounts in local bank and post office. Because of availability of electricity about half of the sampled households have the facility of fan. But the problem of food insecurity may be realized from the fact that only 32 households have food for the entire year. The remaining are hand to mouth and regularly they have to manage food items, and most of them manage it through wage work.

Of course, electricity has encouraged many of them to adopt modern means of entertainment, but they are far away from the basic facility of toilet, tap water and newspaper. Toilet and tap water is not available even in a single household. Only 2 of the households subscribe newspaper. Similarly, the number of users of motorized vehicle is also insignificant. This is clear from Table 2.12.

Table 2.12 : Household and Agricultural Assets

Household Assets

Items	*Total*	*Yes*	*%*	*No*	*%*
Electricity	200	197	98	3	2
Telephone	200	0	0	200	100
Television	200	61	31	139	70
Radio/Tape recorder	200	86	43	114	57
Two Wheeler	200	13	7	187	94
Latrine	200	0	0	200	100
Sewing Machine	200	3	1	197	99
Bank/Post Office Account	200	47	24	153	77
Grain Storage	200	17	9	183	92
Cooler/Fan	200	102	51	98	49
Refrigerator	200	0	0	200	100
Four Wheeler	200	0	0	200	100

(Contd.)

Table 2.12 (Contd.)

Tap Water	200	0	0	200	100
Newspaper	200	2	1	198	99
Food for whole year	200	32	16	168	84
Drawing room	200	3	1	197	99

Agricultural Assets and Cattle

Items	*Total*	*Yes*	*%*	*No*	*%*
Tractor	200	0	0	200	100
Thresher	200	2	1	198	99
Sprayer	200	14	7	186	93
Cow/Buffalo	200	121	61	79	40
Goat	200	33	17	167	84
Tube-well	200	5	3	195	98
Ox/Plough	200	18	9	182	91
Bullock cart	200	12	6	188	94

Agricultural Assets

Since the respondents possess small amount of land and traditionally before the allotment of land to them under the *Charnoi* scheme most of them were landless, therefore, the number of modern agricultural instruments like tractor, thresher, harvester and tube well etc. is by and large not available with them. At the same time only few of them have cattle and bullock cart. Seventeen per cent households of course possess goats. Cow and buffalo is available with more than 60 per cent households.

III

Land Allotment

It is true that land is a physical entity, but it has different meanings. For some it is a source of livelihood but for others it is a source of prestige and power. Hence cross-section of people depending upon their social background define land in their own way. Neale (1971) said that in the European tradition there are at least three distinct social meanings attributed to the term land, i.e. (a) there is land as an area to be farmed, (b) there is land as the sum total of natural resources, which is the economists views of land, and (c) there is land as the area over which a political sovereign wield power. In the current study we are concerned with all the three meanings of land. Maine (1876) has highlighted the political/administrative meaning of land. To him land has been the source of power in Rome and pre-British India due to the following reasons:

> "Land to the early Romans was one of a number of items which made up the family, or class under the authority of the Peter families. The family was a sovereignty–later a sub-sovereignty- defined in sociological terms, that is interactions of its members with members of other families occurred through the agency of the Peter families, these interactions frequently involving decisions to use or augment power; our idea of land as territory-to-role is derived from this aspect of early Roman law and become explicitly political as the state superseded the Peter families. Land in pre-British Indian society was one of the aspects of rulership whether viewed in the person of a *raja*, in the body corporate of a *bhaichara* (brotherhood), village, or in the person of the *Zamindar*, the closest approximation to the Peter families. Then the Indian view of land was also political if we may call a view political when it embraces more than does our concept of politics."

In Indian society, particularly among the Hindus, for centuries, and more specifically upto the end of British Raj land was perceived as "mother". It was not perceived as commodity. Therefore, it was not subject to purchase and sale. Those who had to sale land under the stress solution they perceived themselves unfortunate. Gradually due to various reasons land came in the market and it became commodity in the villages. Bailey (1957) rightly said: "The limitations of the environment, natural growth of the population and growth by immigrations, the presence of capital to invest, the profits of investing in rice land and tobacco land and the absence of investment avenues, other than in land," were the factors responsible for bringing land in the market. As usual land is still the main and for many the only source of livelihood. But many of them of course live in the villages but they do not own land. They work on other's land simply as wage earner, and in many cases they are even not paid as per the minimum wages acts. Majority of these wage earners in the villages are from the marginalized sections. Government of M.P. decided to allot land to them for their ensured livelihood. It was assumed that of 5 per cent grazing land available in the villages upto 3 per cent of it may be allotted to the poor dalits. This package will create new ray of hope initially in the economic life and subsequently in other walks of life. How the beneficiaries came to know about it? On what bases lands were allotted to them? Did they got possession of the allotted land? What are the difficulties which the allottees had to experience in course of possession? And, what are their feelings about allotment of land? These are some of the broad issues covered in the following pages.

Allotment of Land

Respondents received news about allotment of grazing land available in their own villages among them from different sources, i.e. both formal and informal. However, role of *patwari* and *panchayat* was very significant. 44 and 24 per cent respondents received information through these *patwaris* and *sarpanchs* respectively. The role of village watchmen was also important. However, only 14 per cent respondents received the news through villagers and family/caste fellows. Two respondents knew about it from the SDM office. Hence, it is evident that for majority formal source of information particularly operating at the local level was crucial for more than 75 per cent respondents.

Amount of Land Allotted

Majority of the respondents (57%) were allotted less than 2.5 acres of land. The remaining were allotted either or more than 2.5 acres of land. Actually 34 per cent households were allotted more than 2.5 acres of land. This is clear from following Table 2.13.

Table 2.13 : Size of Allotted Land

Sl.No.	*Response*	*Frequency*	*%*
1.	Do not know	38	19
2.	Upto 2.5 acres	106	53
3.	Above 2.5 acres	56	28
	Total	**200**	**100**

Effort for Allotment

When the respondents came to know about the scheme they made efforts for allotment. Large number of them (43%) submitted application to the SDM, and received the help of *patwari*. Some of them also approached sarpanch and village Choukidar. Since about 38 per cent had already land under their possession since long, therefore, no specific effort was made by them. They just requested the concerned official to allot the land already with them. And they all succeeded in it. Further, remaining 14 per cent did not make any effort. They were easily and automatically allotted land because they are poor and they do not possess land. After submitting their application majority of the respondents received cooperation from the concerned government officials and the panchayat representatives in the allotment of land. The role of *patwari* was very helpful in the case of 17 per cent respondents.

Possession

In the case of 87 per cent respondents no problem was experienced from any corner while getting possession of land. Only in the case of 10 per cent beneficiaries problem was created by either the entire village, from the non-dalit families and in the case of 2 per cent beneficiaries problem was created by their own caste fellows. Actually land illegally possessed by the rich dalit was allotted to the poor dalit.

All the respondents observed that land was distributed among the deserving people. For 84 per cent respondents it was allotted to the landless family. Fourteen per cent said that land was allotted to those who had already encroached the land. The remaining had land but it was too small to provide livelihood support. Hence, respondents clearly said that land was allotted to the needy and the genuine people. This can also be substantiated from the fact that majority of our respondents are poor and historically landless. They are completely dependent on farming and wage work.

Bases of Allotment

Of course at the policy level both caste and class based indices were taken into consideration while launching the project but at the local level due to logistic reason only economic standing of the beneficiaries were taken into consideration. In 84 per cent cases it was the *patwari* who decided about land allotment. Role of *sarpanch*, S.D.M and others were not very obvious. However, majority of the respondents (75%) received land because they were landless. 12 per cent said that they had already land but since their name was in BPL list so on this basis land was allotted to them. Six per cent had already encroached the government land and since they fulfilled the required criteria, therefore, land was allotted to them. Two respondents received land through lottery method because the number of the expected beneficiaries was larger than the availability of land. Genuineness of this project may be realised from the fact that majority of the allottees (94%) covered in our study were landless since long.

Table 2.14 : Landholding Size of the Beneficiaries before Allotment

Sl.No	*Response*	*Total*	*%*
1.	Legally landless	187	94
2.	Less than 2.5 acres	10	5
3.	2.5 acres	1	1
4.	Above 2.5 acres	2	1
	Total	**200**	**100**

It may be said that in the area under study majority of the beneficiaries were from the category I, i.e. landless dalits although significant number of them had already encroached the land. Hence, benefit of allotment of *Charnoi* land has really been availed by the poorest from among the poor dalits. On this basis it may be said that in agrarian history of M.P. it is for the first time than in the real sense land was made available to the poor dalits.

Obtaining *Patta*

Many of the allottees (44%) received land *Patta* and other related paper within a month but many (47%) had to wait for months. Actually they received *patta* after three months. But as reported by them, in spite of delay none of them faced difficulty in receiving *patta*. The only constraint which they experienced was related to time. And, of course, some of them had to visit *patwari* and the concerned office again and again to obtain land related papers.

The respondents perceived this constraint in an usual way. They have experience of visiting the change agent times and again even without any substantial gain.

Location and Quality of Land

All the respondents know the location and whereabouts of land. As a result, they have clear idea about its quality. While 39 per cent perceive land as of good quality and most of them are those who have been allotted those lands which were in their possession since long. For 8 per cent it is of bad quality. For the remaining 54 per cent the quality of land is average. Actually they are of the view that after doing cleaning/ploughing/levelling work for a couple of years the quality of land will improve. Hence, by and large beneficiaries have positive opinion about the quality of land allotted to them.

Alternative of Land

Land is still the most beloved source of livelihood among the poor dalits. This may be realised from the fact that in response to a question that which one they prefer most either land, money or job, 57 per cent opted only land. This is because for its use and management neither they have to go out nor they need specific training, of course, they need economic support to manage land properly. Forty-three per cent said that in case of choice they might have preferred money. This is because they might have engaged themselves in non-agricultural activities. Only a single respondent preferred government job. This shows that poor dalits living in the villages do not have inclination in favour of government job. They wish to engage themselves only in primary sector activities.

IV

Status and Features of Allotted Land

Land is the major source of livelihood for majority of the poor dalits in villages. However, allotment of land is a necessary condition and not sufficient condition to fulfil their basic requirement and strengthen the strategy to overcome out of the trap of poverty. It is also essential that besides other inputs the quality of land should also be proper and land should not be under dispute. The farmers should feel that they are permanent owner of the land and whatever they get out of cultivation it is only owned by them and neither owned nor shared by others. Women of such families also do farm work. Till date they had no ownership of land. Under the present scheme arrangement was made to ensure name of both husband and wife on the land *patta*. This effort has been made to empower the poor women. The role of panchayat/government and society at large is required to ensure effective functioning of the allotted land. What are the grassroot level reality on these issues? This part of the chapter deals with all these issues.

Quality of Allotted Land

Location of land in terms of distance is very near in the case of 53 per cent beneficiaries. The allotted land is located within the distance of 1 km. from their house. But in the case of remaining 47 per cent respondents the allotted land is located at a distance of more than 1 km. Similarly, majority of the respondents (93%) have received a single piece of land. Availability of proper amount of land and viability of larger size of land was perhaps the reason behind this action. Respondents at large perceived single piece of land in a larger size positively.

Quality of land is very crucial. Respondents had mixed reaction on this question. For majority (59 per cent) it was plain and levelled. However, for 36 and 10 per cent it was rocky and deep respectively. This is clear from Table 2.15.

Table: 2.15 : Quality of allotted land (Single response)

Sl.No.	*Quality*	*Total*	*%*
1.	Rocky	71	36
2.	Plain	109	55
3.	Full of trenches	20	10
Total	**200**	**200**	**100**

Of the 55 per cent who perceived their land plain, majority of them were using the land since long without legal authority. These lands were allotted to them. They had developed the land during last several years. They are extremely happy that the land already cultivated by them have been allotted to them.

Many of the beneficiaries have done effort to make the allotted land cultivable and beneficial. While 40 per cent had encroached the land in past hence after legal allotment they had not to do any additional effort. Many of the remaining had to do specific effort. For instance, 17 per cent had to do ploughing and levelling work on constant basis, but 14 per cent did not make any specific effort as yet. The remaining have simultaneously done cleaning, ploughing and levelling work. This is clear from Table 2.16.

Table: 2.16 : Effort to Make Land Useful (Single Response)

Sl.No.	*Response*	*Total*	*%*
1.	No response	5	2.5
2.	Ploughing/levelling	34	17
3.	No effort as yet	37	18.5
4.	Only cleaning	27	13.5
5.	Encroached land allotted	79	39.5
6.	2+4	18	9
	Total	**200**	**100**

Help from Government

Government is already aware about economic limitation of these people. Therefore, in the document of *Dalit Agenda* itself it was promised that besides land they will also be provided input both in cash and kind. An attempt was made by the Government of M.P. to fulfil this promise. This is evident from the fact that 66 per cent beneficiaries have received government support. While 33 per cent received monetary support, 22 per cent received grain and the remaining received both cash and grain. The remaining 44 per cent received nothing. In course of our study it was observed that large number of even those respondents received help who were not supposed to improve their land because since long land was under their control and over the time due to their own effort they had improved its quality. Hence, for the purpose of improvement of land they were not entitled to avail this package. It would have been better had their share been distributed among those who have been for the first time allotted the land and who are actually in the situation of hand to the month and they really need help.

Irrigation

It is needless to mention that in the normal situation also there is water problem in this district. 91 per cent respondents do not have any facility to irrigate the allotted land. They have to cultivate land and earn their livelihood without irrigation. The remaining have the facility of duck well, tank, river and tube well which they may use with other's cooperation. This problem may be attempted partly by providing big tank facility under the Rajiv Gandhi Watershed Mission and partly by encouraging less irrigation centred crops.

Encroachment

Many (31) respondents said that at the time of allotment the land allotted to them was under the possession of others. Most of these "others" were non-dalits. But in course of getting possession only few had to face rough weather. They informed the police and time and again visited the police to get possession of the land. Of 31, 22 had to report the matter to police, and the remaining 5 reported to *tehsildar*. The others did not make any effort. It is needless to mention that role of police in the eviction of the encroached land was significant. Actually they adopted persuasive technique with the help of *tehsildar*, panchayat representatives and others and convinced the encroachers to vacate the land. But it is needless to mention that land allotted to 13 households in our sampled villages are still encroached by the village influentials who are from the other Backward Classes.

Difficulties in Approaching the Land

As stated earlier, in many cases allottees have received land at a distant place, therefore, many of them have to face problem while going to their own land. In fact 18 per cent respondents face such difficulties. These difficulties are only because of distance and lack of approaching path. Therefore, they said that either they may be allowed to approach the land through other's land or in exceptional cases instead of the allotted land other land may be allotted where one can early reach and can work even in the early morning or evening hours. In that case it would be safe for women to assist family members on land.

Women and Land Allotment

There was an instruction from the government that *patta* of *Charnoi* land provided to the beneficiaries must be joint and it should be owned by both husband and wife. This decision was taken to ensure share of women in property which is historically owned by only men. It was assumed that through this effort empowerment of women can be made. This effort succeeded here. This is because in the case of 74 per cent respondents there is joint *patta*. In 3 per cent cases *patta* is only owned by women because there is no adult male member and in the remaining 23 per cent cases partly because of unawareness and partly due to lack of women in the family, *patta* was issued to male members, In few cases this instruction was ignored by patwari himself. In other cases allottees are either unmarried or their wife is dead.

Whether there is name of women on *patta* or not, they are associated with land and they are bound to share gains and pains related to land. Of course, in the case of 60 per cent households there is no impact of allotment of land on the status of women because the period of allotment is very short at this level, but in the case of remaining 40 per cent respondents there is visible impact. This is clear form the following table.

Table 2.17 : Impact of Land Allotment on Women (Single Response)

Sl.No	*Response*	*Frequency*	*%*
1.	No impact as yet	119	60
2.	Wage work decreased	3	2
3.	Social status increased	14	7
4.	Women are more happy	35	18
5.	Now concentrate on own land	22	11
6.	2+5	1	1
7.	4+5	6	3
	Total	**200**	**100**

Table 2.17 clearly shows that 3 per cent women now either do not go for wage or they rarely go. This is because about 11 per

cent women now concentrate on their own land. In the case of 7 per cent households there is improvement in social status of women. In 18 per cent households today women are more happy. In the remaining households women have experienced more than one benefit out of *Charnoi* land allotted to their families. In other words, about 40 per cent beneficiaries perceived positive impact of land on women. Most of the interviewees were however men.

As farming is joint exercise among family members in terms of both age and sex, therefore, it is assumed that women and children are doing significant role in managing the land for cultivation purpose. This assumption was confirmed in this study. This is because only in 9 per cent households women and children have not done any work in this direction. But in the case of 89 per cent households both women and children have helped the male elders in cleaning work. In 2 households they are interested to go on farm but due to lack of approaching path they are unable to assist the family members. In the case of remaining households women are helping by protecting crop from cattle, birds and wild animals.

Pains of Land Allotment

Because of allotment and possession of *Charnoi* land large number of respondents and the family members experience tension although the nature of tension is serious in only few cases. While 46 per cent do not experience any loss, 29 per cent have already spent all their saving in the preparation of land and subsequent harvesting work. Five per cent respondents suffered mental tension and 2 households had to spent money in reporting the matter against the encroachers. Two households are now no more in talking term with the encroacher whose land was allotted to them. Nine per cent beneficiaries had to visit *tehsil* office again and again right from the level of submitting application for allotment till getting possession of land and financial support. At all the levels they had to spent both time and money. Some respondents (7%) admitted that they had to bribe *patwari* and *sarpanch* for allotment and possession of land. The remaining 7 respondents shared more than one difficulties. This is clear from Table 2.18.

Table 2.18 : Difficulties (Single Response)

Sl.No.	*Response*	*Frequency*	*%*
1.	Spent money in land preparation	59	29
2.	No loss	91	46
3.	Suffered mental tension	11	5
4.	Spent money in reporting	3	1
5.	No talking term with encroacher	2	1
6.	Spent money in visiting tehsil again and again	19	9
7.	Cash given to patwari/sarpanch	15	7
	Total	200	**100**

Land Allotment

All the respondents said that land allotted to them are *Charnoi* since long and none of them were allotted land owned by the department of the forest. All the respondents including the encroachers have legally received government land for the first time. They neither know any scheme which was introduced in the past for land to the landless dalits nor they have received any benefit out of these schemes.

In the study it was observed that 61 households had encroached government land at different point of time and they were cultivating it. All of them ware allotted the land under this scheme. The remaining 139 were allotted fresh land.

Caste Conflict

As stated, this study was conducted in 13 villages. In none of these villages land related serious caste conflict took place. However, in one of the neighbouring Sat Pipaliya village violent conflict took place which took one life. Details of the case is mentioned below.

Sat Pipaliya located at the distance of 10 km. from Sehore town is an underdeveloped village like other neighbouring villages.

During the rainy season it is difficult to reach the village. The village is numerically dominated by Dalits (*Balai*) and OBC (*Khati*) population. The population size of the village is 1200. During 2002, 36 Dalit families were allotted *Charnoi* land. Most of these lands were under the possession and control of a section of *Khati* families. Each of the allottees were allotted 3 acres of land. Although due to intervention by the administration the encroachers were forced to vacate the land, but they were angry with the decision. They were not mentally and socially prepared to see that the land used by them is allotted to and owned by the landless dalit. As a result, even on minor issue conflict took place between two caste groups on June 30, 2003 in which 16 dalits received injury of which one person died. FIR was lodged against 13 people and most of them are in jail today (*Dainik Bhaskar*, dated 1.7.2003)

Inter-Caste Relation

There was an apprehension in media and others that because of distribution of *Charnoi* land among dalits purely on caste consideration. There will be hostile relation between both rich and poor in the villages. The poor non-dalits will feel isolation because in spite of being poor they are away from the land package only because they are non-dalit. The rich will perceive it as a threat and challenge. They perceive that those who are working on their land and are dependent for various purposes will raise their head and will interact in an equal manner. Therefore, violence was apprehended by some at the very outset of this project. But this apprehension did not became true. This is because 84 per cent beneficiaries feel that their relations with non-dalits are as usual. They are as intimately related to non-dalits as they were in the past. The remaining 16 per cent respondents of course said that because of this scheme the nature of inter-caste and inter personal relation is not as smooth as it was in the past. They said that some disliked this project, therefore, dislike the beneficiaries. Some said that there is direct clash with the non-dalits. Five per cent said that since the land encroached by others, both dalit and non-dalit were allotted to them, therefore, there is clash of interest with them. This is clear from Table 2.19.

Table 2.19 : Land Distribution and Inter-caste Relation (Single Response)

Sl.No.	*Response*	*Frequency*	*%*
1.	No impact/as usual	155	78
2.	Clash	1	1
3.	Some disliked it	9	5
4.	Difference emerged	7	4
5.	They disliked land scheme for dalit	7	4
6.	Smooth relation with all	12	6
7.	Hostile with encroachers only	9	5
	Total	200	**100**

Table 2.19 clearly reflects that this project did not invite tension and conflict in the villages as it was apprehended. Only difference of opinion emerged in a section of villagers. This is perhaps because people at large perceived this project in proper way, and also because they might have realized that just by allotting poor or ordinary quality of land to the resourceless dalits in an area where there is serious irrigation problem, government cannot improve bargaining power of the allottees and therefore, the later cannot change and challenge social and political hegemony of either the upper castes or the other backwards classes. Therefore, there was no sharp reaction against this project in most of the villages.

V

Use of Land and Its Impact

Depending upon the level of technological modernization at the community level and access to these facilities at the individual/ group level as well as amount of exposure to outside world the nature and type of use of agricultural land is determined. If the land is under cultivation since recently, if the cultivator is poor, if there is no proper irrigation and other modern facility, there is possibility of cultivation of single crop. Also, given the situation production for market or production of cash crop is not possible. But this does not mean that there is no change in social and economic status, psychology, mind set and interpersonal relationship among the landowners. If a poor and landless person is provided land along with ownership of land right there is possibility of socio-economic change in life. How and to what extent change takes place? How the beneficiaries perceive it? These are some of the broad issues discussed in this section of the paper.

Use of Allotted Land

Of course, land was allotted in the middle or just before middle of 2002 but they got its physical possession in the due course. In many cases it took more than a month. Also, amount of rain fall during 2002 was very low. Besides, due to poor quality of land many had to wait for months to make it useful and beneficial. As a result, about half of the beneficiaries did not use the land and therefore, no crop was produced during last year. But during 2003 partly because of proper rain fall and partly due to improvement in the quality of land within one year, half of the respondents used the land and they produced some of the major crops. However, *soya* and *jawar* was the most preferred crop yielded. Wheat was also yielded by some of the respondents. Since many of them had for the first time cultivated that particular allotted land therefore, quality of crop was not upto the mark. However, farming was successful in those lands which were under cultivation since long through encroachment. This is clear from Table 2.20.

Table 2.20 : Major Crop Yielded in 2002

Sl. No.	*Response*	*Frequency*	*%*
1.	No cropping/No possession till date	97	49
2.	Maize, Soya, Wheat, Pulse	3	2
3.	Soya, Maize, Wheat	6	3
4.	Soya, Jawar, Maize, Tuar	8	4
5.	Soya, Wheat	7	4
6.	Soya, Maize, Tilli	9	5
7.	Soya, Jawar	31	16
8.	Wheat	7	4

(Contd.)

Table 2.20 *(Contd.)*

Sl. No.	*Response*	*Frequency*	*%*
9.	First time cultivated land	8	4
10.	Soya	6	3
11.	Crop was bad	2	1
12.	Soya, Wheat, Jawar	8	4
13.	Wheat, Soya, Jawar, Maize, Red Tuar	7	4
14.	Soya, Maize	1	1
	Total	**200**	**100**

Currently all the respondents who were allotted land are by and large using it. Except one respondent they all have sown crop and they are also satisfied with it. Some of the common crop shown are *jawar, maize, soya, tilli* and *peanuts*. This is clear from Table 2.21.

Table 2.21 : Standing crop during 2003

S.No.	Response	Frequency	%
1.	No cropping due to lack of approaching road	1	1
2.	Jawar, Maize,.Soya	28	14
3.	Soya	41	21
4.	Soya, Jawar	41	21
5.	Soya, Maize, Tuar	7	4
6.	Jawar, Turaw, Tilli	1	1
7.	Maize, Soya	21	11
8.	Peanuts, Jawar	28	14
9.	Peanuts, Maize	12	6
10.	Jawar, Maize	8	4
11.	Jawar	4	2
12.	Peanuts	8	4
	Total	**200**	**100**

On the basis of Tables 2.20 and 2.21 it is clear that of course initially most of the allotted land was properly not used, but during 2003 the land was under possession, any dispute related to land was over, people had already received financial support from government and there was heavy rain fall. As a result of these combined forces, almost the entire land was under cultivation. Quality of some of the standing crops was excellent. However, in all the cases only those crops were yielded which are yielded in the area under study. New variety crop was not attempted.

Psychological, Social and Economic Impact

Whether the respondents received land for the first time or land which was already under their cultivation and it was allotted to them, in the case of both, the news of allotment of land was very pleasant and joyful for all the respondents. Some said that it was even out of their imagination to become land owner (Choudhary; 2005).

But since land was allotted to them only few months ago, therefore, its economic impact was yet not visible in the case of many respondents. In other words, 58 per cent do not see its economic impact at this point of time. But 7 per cent said that they have harvested crop and it is sufficient for their consumption for at least 3 months. Six per cent said that they have just started cropping work so that they cannot assess its economic impact. Seven per cent have yielded food grain which is sufficient for more than 6 months. Twenty-two per cent feel that today in comparison to past their economic standing is relatively better. This is clear from Table 2.22.

Table 2.22 : Economic Gain

Sl.No.	*Response*	*Frequency*	*%*
1.	No impact as yet	115	58
2.	Sufficient for three months	13	7
3.	Cropping for first time	11	6
4.	Land received recently	5	3
5.	Sufficient for six months	13	7
6.	Better than past	43	22
	Total	**200**	**100**

But people at large (64%) do not see any improvement in their social status. They do not feel that now they are respected more incomparison to the past. This is because many people like them have been allotted land and the allotted land has yet to demonstrate its economic impact. But in contrary to this 15 per cent said that now they themselves as well as their neighbour perceive them as land owner. Twenty per cent also feel that their status has improved and the local *sahukar* do not hesitate to advance them loan or food items on credit, because they perceive that our economic status have improved and we will definitely return the debt. Similarly, women do not go on others land for wage works. Now many of them concentrate on their own land. This is improvement in status. Few respondents feel that it has both positive and negative impact.

Land was allotted to them to overcome the trauma of poverty. All the respondents also perceived it in the similar manner. Many of them said that by doing hard labour, increasing income and saving, proper cultivation, better cropping and both the cultivation and wage work, they will deal with the problem of poverty. Besides this, some of the respondents said that land, which will lead to more than one opportunity, will definitely help them to come out of the trap of poverty. This is clear from Table 2.23.

Table 2.23 : Role of Land in Poverty Alleviation (Single Response)

Sl.No.	*Response*	*Frequency*	*%*
1.	Not applicable	2	1
2.	By hard labour	93	46.5
3.	By better cropping	14	7
4.	By cultivation and wage work	6	3
5.	Not to purchase grain	6	3
6.	By proper cultivation	6	3
7.	By increasing income	12	6
8.	Saving	61	30.5
	Total	**200**	**100**

Dalit's Perception about Perception of Others

Respondents were asked to map perception of others such as those dalits who did not receive land, *sarpanch* and non-dalits about the scheme of allotment of land to them and various issues related to it. In response to this, mixed opinions were expressed. For example, 74 per cent said that the non-dalits do not bother on this issue. In contrary to this 3 per cent were very angry because now they have to face grazing problem. Others said that non-dalits have negative views on this issue. They became jealous and they disliked this project because of their own vested interest.

But in contrary to this 50 per cent dalits, who were not allotted land, they feel that it should also be allotted to them. Thirty-six per cent feel that dalits do not think on this issue, but for 13 per cent since every dalit in their village received land, therefore, their perception as an outsider on the issue of allotment of land does not arise.

Sarpanch at large do not think on these issues. This was observed by 62 per cent respondents. But 24 per cent said that they are positive on this issue and it is they who helped dalits to get benefit out of this project. Except few, the remaining others praised the role of *sarpanch* in the total process of allotment and possession of land.

On this basis it seems that majority of the respondents feel that reaction of others are mixed. They do not think on this, if they are non-dalit, some of them are jealous. If they are dalits many of them opined that they should also be allotted land.

Migration

It is assumed that as the job opportunity will increase at the native place, the poor at large will not make involuntary migration. They perceive migration in a painful manner and in many cases if they do not see livelihood support system they migrate. It is observed that 43 per cent feel that even today they go outside the village for wage. But this is not migration. They go out in the morning and come back in the evening. Thirty-three per cent said that now they seldom go out for work. Eighteen per cent said that they also go for others work within and outside the village only when they have no work on their own land. On this basis it is clear that of course frequency of spacial mobility either just outside the village or at distant places will definitely come down but it will not discontinue completely. This is because looking to the size of land, poor economic condition and lack of irrigation facility, respondents have to search more than one source of income and livelihood. This source may be wage work within the village or outside it. But it is sure that the amount of wage work will definitely decrease and they will concentrate on their own land which was not possible in the past particularly in the case of those respondents who have just received land.

Hence, it is evident that during 2002, i.e. the year of allotment many of the respondents did not use the land allotted to them. Some of them used but the condition of their crop was not upto the mark. However, they had psychological satisfaction that they are landowners. But during 2003 the status of standing crop is much better. Most of the beneficiaries have cultivated the land. However, in both the years they have produced traditional crop. They feel that land allotted to them will help them to come out of the trap of poverty. This will also lead to reduction in the frequency of seasonal involuntary migration.

VI

Other's Perceptions

In order to maintain objectivity and neutrality in the study it is essential that opinions expressed by respondents must be verified from different sources. One among these is a section of population who are otherwise not related to the issue under study, but who keep eye on these issues and who also knows respondents since quite some time. For this purpose in course of our study in 13 villages we decided to seek the opinions of at least 2 persons from each of the 13 villages, to know their perceptions about dalit-*Charnoi* land interface. These respondents are local, they are both dalit and non-dalit and many of them also hold some formal position and command respect in the locality.

Profile of the Key Informants

In terms of caste, we identified respondents from all the caste groups. For instance, 3, 15, 7 and 1 respondents, who were interviewed,

Table 2.24 : Social Background of Respondents

Caste	*General*	*OBC*	*SC/ST*	*Others*	*Total*
Freq.	3	15	7	1	26
%	12	58	27	4	100

Period of Residence	*Since Birth*	*Less than 10 Years*	*More than 10 Years*	*Total*
Freq.	23	0	3	26
%	88	0	12	100

Social Status	*Panch*	*Sarpanch*	*Dy. Sarpanch*	*Panchayat Secretary*	*Rich Dalit*	*Rich Non-dalit*	*Teacher*	*Total*
Freq.	13	4	1	3	1	3	1	26
%	50	15	4	12	4	12	4	100

are from General, OBC, SC/ST and other community (Muslim) respectively. Eighty-eight per cent are living in that particular village since their birth and the remaining 12 per cent, particularly the school teacher, or the Panchayat Secretary, are also living since more than 10 years.

So far as their social status and social position is concerned half of them are *panch*, 4 *sarpanch* and 1 deputy *sarpanch* 3 Panchayat Secretaries were also interviewed. At the same time we could interview 4 rich persons in which one was dalit. Also, 1 teacher participated in the study.

In specific terms, we asked them questions related to the appropriateness of the distribution of the *Charnoi* land to the needy, process of receiving possession, quality of distributed land, inter-personal relationship and impact of land on their social and economic life. Some of the major observations and findings are presented below.

Allotment of Land and its Management

Majority of the respondents feel that *Charnoi* land was distributed among the genuine and needy person. They also said that majority of the allottees have already occupied the allotted land. Some of them have still to occupy the allotted land. This is because the land allotted to them are occupied by others, since long. One respondent said that the allottees have submitted application for the proper exchange of land allotted to him.

Respondents have mixed opinion about the role of *Gram panchayat* in the allotment and possession of land. Forty-two per cent however, do not see role of *panchayat* in this context, but the remaining 12 respondents admitted the role of *panchayat* in this context. They said that by convincing the encroacher to vacate the allotted land, by informing concerned people about the distribution of *Charnoi* land, by seeking help from police and administration for the possession of land and by lodging complaint in *tehsil* office against the encroacher, *panchayat* helped to ensure successful possession of the allotted land to the allottee. Twelve per cent respondents said that since the allotted land was already under possession of the allottee, therefore, in this case there was no role of *panchayat*.

Respondents suggested some measures to ensure successful possession of the land. They said that for this purpose the government should first vacate the land for allotment, public awareness programme should be launched, help of police should also be taken as and when required. Three respondents suggested that if the encroachers are poor, they should also be compensated while taking land back from them, no matter from which caste or caste group they belong. All the respondents perceived that land related papers have already been received by beneficiaries.

Half of the respondents see the allotted land controversial and uncultivable and half not. Those who perceive it in a negative sense, say that if controversial land is not allotted or allotted only after taking it back from the encroachers and if government owned proper or cultivable land is distributed then only land related problems can be sorted out. Two respondents said that it is the *panchayat* which should solve the difference in consultation with both the concerned parties.

Respondents also expressed their awareness regarding the package provided by the government for proper management of the allotted land. For instance, 20 respondents said that allottees have been given seed, money or both to manage their land in a proper way.

Impact

It is apprehended by a section of researchers and media that distribution of *Charnoi* land to the poor dalits and tribals have promoted rural violence and caste tension in different parts of M.P. Logically and on the basis of some cases of violence here and there the allegation seems correct. There are examples in history from different parts of the country that after independence as and when either at its own or due to pressure provincial government made effort to abolish *zamindari* system, introduce land ceiling acts, minimum wages acts etc., land owners individually and in group successfully or unsuccessfully made effort to frustrate the move. But in case of our study 62 per cent respondents observed that the nature of inter-caste relationship is as usual. Twenty-three per cent said that if the encroacher is non-dalit then only relationship is hostile with the allottees, but 15 per cent respondents said that there is hostile relationship between the allottees and rest of the village population in the light of the distribution of *Charnoi* land. In other words, most of our key informants do not see existence of caste conflict or rural violence due to allotment of *Charnoi* land.

All the respondents feel that there is positive impact of allotment of *Charnoi* land on social and economic status of the beneficiaries. Thirty-one per cent said that it has improved their economic status. For 1 respondent now the dalits call themselves farmer, 35 per cent said that now instead of going on other's land they prefer to work on their own land. Some respondents said that they are now landowner. The remaining 4 observed more than one benefit out of this project. This is clear from Table 2.25.

Table 2.25 : Social and Economic Impact (Single Response)

Sl.No.	*Response*	*Frequency*	*%*
1.	It has improved income	10	31
2.	Now they are called farmer	7	4
3.	They will do labour on their own land	9	35
	Total	**26**	**100**

Of course, land to the poor and landless dalit in the villages by the government is very important institutional intervention for their social and economic improvement but it is not a sufficient condition. They should be provided other inputs also so that land can properly be utilized and development process can be made sustainable. Respondents in large number have suggested more than one effort. This is clear from Table 2.26.

Eight respondents said that without irrigation facility land cannot be properly used. One respondent suggested for economic support on constant basis. One respondent said that some more land should be allotted to them. Respondents at large, who made more than one observation, said that if job, loan, regular wage work, fertilizer and seed on proper rate, etc., are provided or made available, Dalits at large can make maximum benefit out of the project. Few respondents also demanded removal of untouchability in this context.

Table 2.26 : Besides Allotting Land Other Efforts to Improve Social and Economic Status of Dalit (Single Response)

Sl.No.	*Response*	*Frequency*	*%*
1.	Non-controversial and good quality land should be allotted	5	19
2.	Irrigation facility should be provided	8	31
3.	Untouchability should be removed	1	4
4.	Job	2	8
5.	Loan	2	8
6.	Regular wage work	2	8
7.	Proper price of food grains	2	8
8.	Economic support	1	4
9.	Fertilizer/seed on subsidized rate	2	8
10.	Some more land should be allotted	1	4
	Total	**26**	**100**

VII

Five Beneficiaries

Case study is one of the qualitative techniques which provide indepath information and insight related to subject under study. Actually it is different to other techniques of data collection which are relatively more methodical and formal, but this technique is more informal and it provides as much detailed and intensive information as it can. In this study, we selected 5 households belonging to 5 different villages of Sehore Development Block. Details of these cases are clear from Table. 2.27.

More Singh

More Singh is *Balai* by caste, who lives in Sonda village. There are about 127 households in the village of which 47 are of Scheduled Castes. There are 5 members in the family. He lives in mixed house and in the past he was landless. The house is electrified and surprisingly today he has television, radio and fan facility.

Table: 2.27 : Demography of Persons Covered for Case Study

Sl.No.	*Name*	*Sub-caste*	*Land Size Before Allotment*	*Land Size After Allotment*	*Education of Ego*	*Number of Family Member*
1.	More Singh	*Balai*	Landless	2.5 acres	Illiterate	5
2	Kamal Singh	*Balai*	Landless	2.5 acres	Illiterate	6
3	Kewal Singh	*Chamar*	Landless	2.5 acres	Illiterate	4
4	Suraj Bai	*Chamar*	Landless	2.5 acres	Illiterate	5
5	Hari Singh	*Balai*	Landless	2.5 acres	Middle	6

Other household and agricultural assets except buffalo/cow is absent in the family. The family is not under debt. He was allotted land upto 2.5 acres from the scheme during 2002. Currently he is using the land. *Patwari* was helpful in the allotment of land. He did not experience challenge from any source while possessing the land. But he said that if either money or land was to be distributed, he might have preferred cash. More Singh also did not experience difficulty in obtaining land related paper. The quality of land allotted to him is of general type, it is in one piece and it is located at a distance of more than 1 k.m. from his residence. He also received Rs. 1210 to manage the land but the land is not properly used as yet. He reasoned,

> "Land is o.k.. but others do not allow me to go through their land. They create problem. If approaching path is provided. I can definitely use my land and come out of the trap of poverty."

He said that land is very close to river. But only because of lack of approaching path he is unable to use the land. Here, it is needless to mention that at the time of allotment the land was under possession of someone else. He had to report to *patwari* then only it was vacated. Now those who had to vacate the land, they do not allow him to cross their own land to reach the allotted land.

The land paper do not contain name of his wife. This is because *patwari* instructed him not to mention the name of his wife on the paper. He said that since land is not used as yet, therefore, it has not affected the family and women and children in proper manner. His only pain is that he wants approaching path. He narrated that due to distribution of land there is hostile relationship with the landowners. The landowners do not like that poor dalits should be provided land. The main source of livelihood of the family is wage labour. Occasionally, he migrates for livelihood. Till date he has not gained anything out of the allotted land.

Kamal Singh

Kamal Singh lives in Chapri village. There are 83 households in the village of which 29 households are of Scheduled Castes. He is *Balai* by sub-caste. Today the main source of his income is agricultural work. In the past he was landless and because of that only *tehsildar* allotted him 2.5 acres of land. There are five persons in the family. In his house also there is electricity and T.V. although it lack toilet facility. He produced food grain which is sufficient for the entire year. He is under debt but he took loan from bank mainly for agricultural and consumption purpose. He also said that he might have preferred cash instead of land. He said that very easily he received land paper, although it took more than 3 months. Land is in his control and its quality is excellent. It is levelled and also located very near to his house. Government provided about 3.5 quintal of rice and wheat to properly manage the allotted land. Land allotted to him lack irrigation facility. This land was also under control of somebody else and government ensured possession. The land paper includes name of both husband and wife. His wife was also wage earner in the past but now she concentrate on her own land. Till date there is no economic impact of the allotted land because the standing crop is still to be harvested. Today he has planted *jawar* and maize. He said that there is no improvement in his social status. Still he goes for wage work. The relationship with the earlier encroacher is hostile. Due to recently allotted land, he can improve economic condition of the family provided loan and irrigation facility is made available.

Kewal Singh

Kewal Singh is *Chamar* by caste. He belongs to Panch Pipaliya village. The village is relatively big because, there are 116 households of which 40 households are of Scheduled Castes. He lives in *kaccha* house and previously he was also landless. There are four members in family. All are illiterate and main source of livelihood is caste occupation, wage labour and farming. Except electricity, fan, radio and cow, he lacks other household and agricultural asset. The family is under debt. He took loan for consumption purpose. He came to know about land allotment scheme through *patwari. Patwari* helped him to obtain land. He received 2.5 acres of land. He said that besides land nothing is suitable to his family. He received land paper without any trouble. The quality of land is proper, it is under his control, it is located at a distant place and it is also in more than one pieces. Originally one of the pieces was not proper but now he cleaned and levelled it at his own. Till date like others he has not received any support from the government. The land lack irrigation facility. At the time of allotment the land was under "others" possession, but police helped him to obtain the land. But he is also facing the problem of approaching path. He is happy that land has been allotted to him, but the land related paper lack the name of his wife. Actually he do not know who did it and why it was done. But the wife has constantly helped him to level the land. As stated, at the time of allotment the land was encroached. To get its possession he had to repeatedly approach the local police. According to him:

> "Today there is hostile relationship with the early encroacher. He always threaten me. When I received land paper and requested him to vacate the land and also showed land paper to him, he became angry and I was forced to go back. I approached the police and because of them only today I am landowner. I have good relationship with all except that particular family."

He said that during last year he produced *soyabean*, wheat and *jawar* and this year also *soya* and maize is now ready for harvest. Because of farming on new land economic condition has improved. It has also improved social status and now they go for wage work only when they do not have work on their own land.

Suraj Bai

Suraj Bai is *Chamar* by caste. She belongs to Londiya village. The village is small. There are 86 households of which 22 households are of dalit community. She was landless before receiving land under the current scheme. Her house is *kaccha* and it is constructed on government land. There are four family members. She neither own any household asset nor the agricultural asset. But at the same time she is not under debt. The only source of livelihood is wage work. She came to know about land distribution from both villagers and *patwari*. But it was latter who helped her to receive land because, she was landless. Villagers opposed land allotment to her. But without facing much difficulty she received the land.

The quality of land is better. It is levelled, located within 1 km. It is only in a single piece. She had to construct soil boundary to stop soil degradation. This land was not under encroachment. Therefore, for the first time she improved the land for cultivation but due to lack of irrigation facility, she had to face problem. She feels that her status is better in comparison to the past. Her name is also maintained on the land paper. She and children work on land and cleaned it for cultivation. Since the land was not encroached, therefore, nobody opposed her when she got its physical possession. But she recorded that in order to obtain *patta*, she had to visit *tehsil* office several times. During last year she planted soyabean, but due to lack of irrigation, she did not get much out of it. Currently *soya* and *jawar* is the standing crop. She said that even today they have to work as wage labour because land is not capable to provide as per requirement. But she is hopeful that on the basis of hard labour and good rain she will be able to produce more resulting thereby improvement in her economic and social status.

Hari Singh

Hari Singh is *Balai* by caste. He belongs to Chitavaliya Van village. There are 103 households in the village of which more than 50 per cent households (61) are of dalits. Historically, the family was landless and received land only under the current scheme of land distribution. His house is *kaccha* and located on community land. In the past his main source of income was wage work, but now the family is also engaged in agricultural work. The family is under debt. He took loan from local Patel family for marriage purpose. The house is electrified with T.V. and fan facility but do not have other assets.

Hari Singh came to know about this scheme from both *tehsildar* and villagers. He submitted application and because he was landless, therefore, 2.5 acres land was allotted to him. The land allotted to him was encroached by Bhassa Singh. He created some problem. But subsequently land was occupied by Hari Singh. Land is located at close to his house. It is in one piece. But due to lack of irrigation and poor quality of soil, land was not very productive. Woman assist in management of the land. The land was jointly allotted to husband and wife. He did not receive any economic support from government. As a result, he had to invest from his own to manage the land. This year only he has planted *soya* and *jawar*. He and his family members are committed to improve farming work but at the same time he wants support from government to meet expenditure on irrigation and fertilizer.

VIII

Conclusion

In spite of seasonal out-migration and different rural development schemes, particularly related to infrastructural development, land is still the main and in many cases the only source of livelihood for large number of dalit population in villages. Whether they own land or are landless and completely depend on wage work, land is the only source of livelihood. Of course, along with the abolition of zamindari system the trend of land reform was started by the state and subsequently different acts were passed to put ceiling on land in the villages but partly because of lack of social and political will on the part of state machinery and partly due to lack of protest movements by the landless population, land reform policies were seldom translated into action in Madhya Pradesh. The *Sarvodaya* movement also did not do much in this direction. The result was that towards the end of the previous century about 20 per cent dalits were landless and more than that possessed very small amount of land. They were poor and hand to mouths. Development projects, involuntary migration, etc., did not improve life conditions of the poor dalits. However, **Bhopal Declaration** popularly known as **Dalit Agenda** introduced by Government of M.P. in January 2002 is one of the most powerful efforts made by the state to empower dalits irrespective of their economic condition and rural/urban background. There is a provision of land to the landless and near landless dalits. It is reported that during the limited period of only several days more than 5 lakh hectares of land were distributed among the dalits and tribals of all the districts. How the dalits in particular feel about it? Are the land allotted to them really in their possession? How they are interacting with land and perceiving its gains and pains? In other words, how land has affected their mind-set, and social and economic life? These are some of the broad issues in the light of which this study was conducted.

The study was conducted in 13 villages of Sehore Development Block of Sehore district. At first after obtaining list of allottees base line information from each of the dalit and non-dalit households living in all the 13 villages were collected through census method. This helped us to locate the actual beneficiary households. In all the 13 villages we found that out of 460 dalit families 232 had received the allotment. Initially we conducted study on 213 households but subsequently we observed that 13 households had received land paper but not possession. After obtaining preliminary information from them we shifted to the remaining 200 households which have already got possession and who are cultivating the land. We used several types of semi-structured interview schedules to collect information from relevant sources. Some of the salient findings of the study are the following.

I

The study was conducted in mixed and medium size villages of Sehore Development Block. The area in general and the villages understudy in particular are underdeveloped. People at large are dependent on agricultural activities. There is electricity facility as a result modern means of entertainment is available in large number, many farmers have tractors but the process of formation of Social Capital is slow. Only one or two small NGOs are available. The presence of health services, political parties are insignificant. There is nothing like toilet facility in the entire thirteen villages. There are significant number of schools but illiteracy level is low. Poverty level is very high among the dalit households.

More or less similar is the situation with beneficiaries. Most of them are from category I. *Chamar* and *Balai* outnumber the other SC population. Most of them live in the *kaccha* house which they have constructed on their own land. Majority of them are under debt. It is interesting to note that of 200 households electricity facility is available in 197 houses and of which TV is available in 61 households although toilet facility is available not even in a single household. None of them have tractor although cow/buffalo is available with more than 60 per cent households.

Majority of the respondents received information about allotment of land through *patwari* and *sarpanch*. It was the *patwari* in many of the cases who helped them to allot land. Beneficiaries at large did not face problem in case of allotment of land. In 84 per cent cases land was allotted to the landless. They were allotted land because of being landless. However, large number of them received land paper after one month of allotment. Land is still the most preferred source of livelihood. This is evident from the fact that in response to a question majority of them said that they preferred only land and nothing else.

So far as condition and quality of allotted land is concerned for majority of them it is plain. About 40 per cent respondents were allotted the piece of land which was cultivated by them since long, therefore, they had not to do extra effort. Irrigation is the only or the most important problem faced by about 90 per cent respondents. In the case of 31 respondents the allotted land was encroached by others. They adopted formal technique to get the land vacated, and they succeeded. In the case of 74 per cent beneficiaries name of both husband and wife is mentioned on *patta*. Women are now more happy and in many cases they now concentrate more on their own land. Both women and children play crucial role in land cleaning work. Only few of the respondents have experienced pain, particularly social tension, due to land allotment. None of them received forest land. In other words, all the respondents were allotted only the *Charnoi* land. And more than 50 per cent received assistance to manage the allotted land. In the case of 78 per cent respondents there is no change in the existing pattern of inter-caste relationship. However, some of the respondents reported that due to allotment of land they are disliked and there is difference of opinions with the villagers if not physical level conflict.

During the middle of 2002 many of the respondents (49%) did not receive land. The remaining received it and cultivated it in time. They produced food grains like maize, *soya*, *wheat*, *jawar*, etc. But during 2003 except one all the respondents cultivated their land. They all produced the common crops. Further, neither during the previous nor during the current year any of them had to face harvest related challenge from any side.

All the respondents had high level psychological satisfaction due to allotment of land. But so far as economic impact is concerned in many of the cases it has to show its impact because they have just started use of the land. However 22 per cent reported that their economic condition is much better than the past. Many of them also remarked that they have now foodgrain for more then 6 months. But people at large do not see improvement in their social status at this point of time. However, all of them feel that they are now land owner and many of them and their women now do not go for wage work. Similarly, majority of the respondents observed that by hard work, better cropping and proper cultivation definitely their income will improve, and they will come above the poverty line. To them only few non-dalits particularly those who have to face now grazing problem, have developed antagonistic relationship with them. At the same time those dalits who did not receive land they expressed desire to receive benefit of allotment of land. Respondents at large said that today there is no much reduction in migration rate but if cultivation work is done properly, it is assumed that seasonal outmigration will definitely be reduced, if not eradicated.

In course of comprehending perception of others such as the key informants from all the 13 selected villages it was observed that land was allotted to the needy and the role of *panchayat* and *patwari* was cooperative and impartial in this context. They said that there was no problem pertaining to possession of land. The condition of encroacher is also poor, therefore, their problem should also be sympathetically heard. Majority of the respondents said that there is positive impact of allotment of land on their social and economic condition. However, they suggested that if alongwith land, irrigation facility is provided, untouchability is removed, job opportunity is created, loan facility is provided, proper price of food grain is provided, some more land is allotted and fertilizer and seed is provided on subsidized rate, of course, condition of poor dalits at large, may be improved.

II

It is a fact that large number of poor and chronically poor particularly in the villages are from the Scheduled Castes. Majority of them either did not own land or they own small amount of land which is incapable to meet their basic requirement for the entire year. As a result, they have partly to depend on wage work and partly on outmigration. But in many cases even these two coping mechanisms are failed to deal with their economic problem. Hence, land to the landless dalit under **Bhopal Declaration** is a historical intervention on the part of the State Government of M.P. Only on the basis of this package it can be said that if the state is weak or absent from the scene, plight of the poor cannot be addressed by any organization including NGO and social movement. NGO can produce model but they cannot contribute to social change at the wider level. Similarly, social movements are also subsequently conditioned by primordial social under currents. But is it that just by providing land to the landless in the area where there is strong scarcity of irrigation facility, plight of the poor can be addressed? On the basis of findings of this study it can be safely said that poor dalits require more than land for their improvement. Some of the efforts made in this direction may be of the following type.

1. Majority of the respondents are of the opinion that so long as proper irrigation facility is not provided, beneficiaries at large cannot use the land properly. There is scarcity of irrigation water and if it is, it cannot be purchased by the poor dalits. Hence, it is suggested that under Ra1jiv Gandhi Watershed Mission in each village, if not many, then at least one or two big tank should be constructed. This tank should be constructed

on common land and can be used by community members as per their requirement and understanding among themselves. If the tank is constructed it will create employment opportunity not only at the time of its construction but also in the due course and dalits at large may be encouraged to participate in water based occupation like fishing. Latently, this experiment will also enhance underground watertable and subsequently time saving as well as improvement in health status of the villagers.

2. Significant number of respondents said that they have received small amount of land. If the common land is available in and around the village some more land should be allotted to them. There are number of families with relatively larger number of family members. All have been equally treated. But land should also be distributed as per the family requirement.

3. There are still some landless families or families with having small amount of land. Such families should also be provided land either within the village or outside it.

4. Some respondents observed that they are poor and they cannot properly improve condition of their allotted land just on the basis of some grant received from the government. Therefore, they suggested that before allotment of land it should be properly treated and improved by the government itself.

5. Before allotment of land opinion of beneficiaries should be taken into consideration. People at large do not like those lands which are either rocky, degraded or where it is difficult to reach.

6. Some said that in many cases land were allotted and people got its possession without proper measurement. As a result, some conflicts are reported. Hence, it is suggested that before providing land related document and actual possession of land, proper measurement of land should be made.

7. Some respondents observed that the amount of cash or kind or both provided to them are not sufficient, its amount should be increased, but while increasing the amount government should not allot extra fund rather the grant provided to those

beneficiaries who are illegally managing the land since long and who have been recently allotted land, condition of that land is improved and plain, hence, instead of providing grant to them, it should be allotted to the new beneficiaries.

8. Respondents at large observed that irrigation facility, seed and fertilizer should be provided to them on subsidized rate on constant basis or so long as they are not above the poverty line by their own effort.

9. Some respondents said that it is difficult for them to manage the land because it is located in another village which is more than 1 km. away from the place of their residence. Women and children find difficulty to go and work on these land. Hence, it is suggested that if grazing land is available within the village itself, they should be allotted the land from that part of the land.

10. Besides allotment of land respondents also said that job opportunity at the village level should be created, loan facility from formal sources at the small interest rate should be provided and health facility should be provided at the village level.

11. In course of study it was reported that one beneficiary sold the land after couple of months of allotment. He sold it to meet social expenditure. Hence, a newly made landowner became landless. In order to stop such development proper law should be formulated which can make them owner without right to sale the land.

On the basis of above suggestions it can be said that if properly managed definitely large number of poor dalits will get benefit and subsequently their physical and social quality of life may improve.

References

Bailey, F.G. (1957), *Caste and Economic Frontier: A Village in Highland Orissa,* Manchester: Manchester University Press.

Blomkvist, H. and Ashok Swain (2001), "Investigating Democracy and Social Capital in India", *EPW*, p. 639.

Choudhary, S.N. (2005) : "Grazing Land to Dalits in Madhya Pradesh : Social Opportunity and Political Cost," *The Indian Journal of Social Work*, Vol. 66 Issue 3 pp. 244-261

Maine, H. (1876), *Village Communities in the East and the West*, p.7.

Neale, W.C. (1971): "Land is to Rule" in *Land Control and Social Structure in Indian History* (ed.) R.E. Frykenberg.

Putnam, Robert (1993), *Making Democracy Work Civic Traditions in Modern Italy*, Princeton University Press.

3
Allotment of Grazing Land to Scheduled Castes and Scheduled Tribes under Dalit Agenda in M.P.

– *Y.G Joshi**

The study is based on the primary survey of eighteen villages of Madhya Pradesh, eight representing the tribal villages and ten representing the beneficiaries of Scheduled Castes category. The study was conducted in 2004 to evaluate the programme of land distribution to dalits, undertaken during the year 2002 by the Government of Madhya Pradesh under the '*Bhopal Declaration*'. The study was conducted at the instance of the State Government, by Dr. Babasaheb Ambedkar National Institute of Social Sciences, Mhow. The paper which is based on the above study, is being presented in six sections, namely, the context and objectives, methodology, profile of sampled villages and sample population, programme evaluation, analysis of conflicts, and findings and recommendations.

I

Context and Objectives

Throughout the country, with respect to revenue land, a certain percentage of land is kept reserved for grazing, sports and other community purpose. In Madhya Pradesh, prior to March 1998, such grazing land, called as *Charnoi*, was kept at 7.5 per cent of the village paper area and was classified as government land. However, for long time it was felt by the revenue department that

* Professor, Dr. B.R. Ambedkar National Institute of Social Sciences, Mhow

a very large percentage of this land in most of the villages, classed as grazing land, was under unauthorized cultivation by the encroachers. This practice was continuing for last many years and the encroachers used to pay fine to keep on holding this land under their possession. Keeping in view this ground reality and the social commitment of the State Government, a decision was taken by the State Government on March 4, 1998 to reduce the percentage of grazing land from 7.5 to 5.0 and distribute this surplus land to landless agricultural labourers of SC and ST category. During this phase 1.54 lakh acres of land in the form of 80,470 *pattas* was distributed to SC/ST families.

After this initial experience, the State Government was determined to benefit more landless SC/ST families by distributing surplus *Chornoi* land. On September 19, 2001 the State Government further reduced the *Charnoi* land from 5 per cent to 2 per cent. In the **Bhopal Document,** released on January 2002, the State Government reiterated its commitment to make available agricultural land to all landless agricultural labourers of SC/ST category, either by allotment of this surplus land or by purchasing agricultural land for such allotment. To solve the problem of local resistance and other bottlenecks coming in the way of the execution of the programme, a detailed guideline was issued by the Revenue Department of the Government of M.P. on 2.3.2002 and instructions were issued to complete the process of actual allotment within a time frame of April 14, 2002 to May 31, 2002.

However, with the launching of the programme some conflicts were reported in different parts of the State. While on the one hand, the ruling party applauded the programme as a leap forward towards their commitment to empower the weaker sections, the opposition parties labelled the programme as political propaganda which actually failed to provide any material benefit to the weaker sections, but on the contrary, widened the rift between different sections. To operationalize the programme instructions were issued to the administration to effectively implement the programme and to take appropriate action against the persons who were creating the hindrance.

Being an important programme aimed at uplifting the weaker sections the present study was undertaken with the following objectives :

1.1 Evaluate the implementation of the programme with reference to set norms, and the deviations;

1.2 Assess the net financial benefit accrued to the allottees and to point out the perceived change in the status of the awardees;

1.3 Analyze the conflicts occurred during the implementation of the programme–their genesis and expected outcome in terms of the process of social change; and

1.4 Suggest suitable interventions, both at the policy and implementation level, based on the study.

II

Methodology

Research Design

During pilot study it was felt that besides quantitative details, the problem involved deeper qualitative aspects related to social psyche and the attitude of the implementation agency at the grass-roots level. Therefore, the research design of the proposed study, besides collecting quantitative details, is largely based on 'Naturalistic Enquiry Mode', involving observations, group discussions with various sections, and case studies.

Sampling Frame

Looking at the large spatial coverage and a need to complete the study in a limited time frame and financial resources, it was not possible to stick to a rigorous sampling framework that may lead to statistically valid generalizations.

The selection of the sample villages was multistaged, based on purposive selection. After the village was selected, all the allottees of that village were included in the study, and thus, at this stage there was no sampling. In the villages where the number of allottees were less than15, the shortfall was covered from the adjoining villages.

During pilot study it was felt that besides over-all social phenomena and administrative problems, the quality of land allotted and the community from which the encroached land was got released, were significant factors affecting the conflicts, and therefore, this factor was also kept in mind while making a purposive selection of the villages. Because the scope of the study was Madhya Pradesh, a wider spatial coverage was necessary. Restricting the study to some district would have eroded the credibility of the evaluation.

Taking into account the above criteria the sampling frame was kept as follows:

Step I. Selection of Blocks

(Nine Blocks were selected, 4 from Tribal development block category) and the rest from other category. Selection was random

One from each division, namely Chambal, Gwalior, Ujjain, Indore, Bhopal, Hoshangabad, Sagar, Jabalpur and Rewa.

Step II. Selection of Villages

Two villages from each of the selected blocks, excluding those which had population below 500, were included in the sample. Thus, a total of 18 villages were included in the study, of which 8 were tribal villages. The selection of tribal villages was made from different tribal zones.

Step III. Selection of Respondents

All the awardees of the programme in the sample village were covered, and thus, at this stage there was no sampling. Where the number of allottees in the sample village were less than 15, the shortfall was covered from adjoining villages.

The list of sample villages, household surveyed and the surveyed population has been given in Table 3.1.

Source of Data and Tools

The secondary data at provincial level was collected from Bhopal, while at the block level it was collected from block headquarters.

Looking to the need of adopting a multi-pronged strategy in collecting the information at the grassroots level, the tools used

Table 3.1 : Sample Villages, Surveyed Household and Surveyed Population

Village Code	District	Block	Sample Village	Surveyed Household			Surveyed Population		
				SC	ST	Total	SC	ST	Total
01	Dhar	Nalcha	Nai Baroda	-	20	20	-	106	106
02	Dhar	Nalcha	Golarzhiri	-	19	19	-	122	122
03	Hoshangabad	Bawai	Nagwada	15	-	15	84	-	84
04	Hoshangabad	Bawai	Ganera	15	-	15	77	-	77
05	Sehore	Sehore	Satpiplya	15	-	15	85	-	85
06	Sehore	Sehore	Jattakhedi	15	-	15	88	-	88
07	Ujjain	Ujjain	Karohan	15	-	15	70	-	70
08	Ujjain	Ujjain	Panthpiplya	15	-	15	91	-	91
09	Sagar	Sagar	Sanodha	15	-	15	89	-	89
10	Sagar	Sagar	Gidwani	15	-	15	90	-	90
11	Mandla	Mandla	Ghugra	-	15	15	-	81	81
12	Mandla	Mandla	Hridaynagar	-	15	15	-	64	64
13	Shehdol	Suhagpur	Lalpur	-	15	15	-	109	109
14	Shehdol	Suhagpur	Kotma	-	15	15	-	90	90
15	Chhindwada	Chhindwada	Khunarjhiri	-	15	15	-	93	93
16	Chhindwada	Chhindwada	Mujawarmal	-	15	15	-	94	94
17	Morena	Ambah	Beelpur	15	-	15	125	-	125
18	Morena	Ambah	Joha	15	-	15	100	-	100
	Total			**150**	**129**	**279**	**899**	**759**	**1658**

included observation, group discussions, interview schedules and few case studies.

III

Profile of Sample Village and Surveyed Population

As specified in Section II, 18 villages from nine districts were included in the present survey, out of which 8 were tribal dominated villages. The selection of villages had been purposive, with a consideration of representing diverse conditions from a wider spatial coverage. Amongst the tribal villages too, villages from different tribal zones of the State were included.

The Profile of Sample Villages

1. Nai Baroda

The village Nai Baroda is a multi-caste village from Nalcha tribal block of Dhar district. The approach of the village is from Dhar-Dharmpuri road near Badiphata. Kunjrod and Bherupiplya are adjoining villages. The village is a multi-caste village. Bhils are economically poor class owning less productive agricultural land while *Balai* (SC), *Meena, Thakur* are main land-owning castes of the village. Due to the recently constructed tank in the village there has been a significant increase in the agricultural production.

Nearly 38 *pattas* were distributed in the *panchayat* area. Because nearly all of them were actually holding that land previously, it was only a paper work of legal entitlement, and therefore, no cases of disputes were reported. Most of the land distributed was of poor quality.

2. Golarzhiri

Golarzhiri is a hundred percent tribal village of Dhar district, inhabited by Bhils and Bhilala tribes. The village is 4 km from village Kunjarod, situated on Manpur-Mandav road. Manpur is 21 km. away from Mhow, on the Agra-Mumbai road. In the Golarzhiri panchayat nine villages are included and a total of 78 *pattas* were distributed among ST families. Still 11 landless persons could not get the *patta*, as no land was available. In a majority of the cases, ST themselves were holding the land and only legal entitlement was given to them, as such, there was no resistance. However, wherever the encroachers were from *Khati* caste of OBC the actual possession of land to ST could not materialize. Most of the land distributed to ST was poor class agricultural land.

3. Nagwada

Village Nagwada is a small village of Hoshangabad district, with a population of 1300. The village is 35 km. from Hoshangabad and 13 km. from the block headquarter, Babai. It is easily approachable from Babai, as it is located on Babai-Nasirabad road, on which a number of private jeeps operate at frequent interval. The main land-holding castes of the village are *Meena* and *Yadav* from OBC and *Agrawal* from general category. There were 48 houses of SCs, of which 38 were *Chamar (Ahirwar)* and 10 were *Basod*. Land allotment was made to 32 families within *panchayat*, out of which 25 were from SC and 7 were from ST. Though 75 per cent of the cultivated fields were on level land with fertile black loamy soils, the quality of land distributed to beneficiaries was poor.

4. Ganera

Like Nagwara village, Ganera is also situated 17 km. from Babai block headquarter of Hoshangabad district, on the Babai-Nasirabad road. The village is easily approachable. This village is a small one with a population of 987. Nearly 60 per cent of agricultural land has fertile black loamy soils, 20 per cent has medium quality soils, while the rest has stony or gravely soils. *Yadav* and *Meena,* belonging the OBC and *Agrawal* are the main land-holding castes of the village. Out of 198 household of the village 43 belonged to SC communities, represented by *Chamars* (35), *Basod* (6), and *Kori* (2). Besides, there were 4 households of tribals who resided on the outskirts. In the land distribution programme 24 families were distributed land within *panchayat*, of which 23 were from SC and one from ST.

5. Satpiplya

Satpiplya is a medium-sized village of Sehore block and district. The village is located 8 km. from Sehore, towards Indore, at a distance of 6 km. from the main road. The population of the village was 2500. Out of 475 total household, 350 belong to *Khati Samaj* which is the dominant land-holding caste of the village. Other important communities of the village are *Muslim, Ahirwar, Basod* and *Balai*. The last three of the above communities belong to Scheduled Castes. Nearly 80 per cent of the cultivated area has rich black fertile soils. In the land distribution programme, within *panchayat* area, 31 SC families were allotted land, out of which 3 were *Balai*, 5 were *Basod* and 23 were *Ahirwar*. The village became notorious due to conflicts that occurred due to land distribution programme, resulting in one murder. This event got wide publicity, both in print and electronic media.

6. Jattakhedi

Jattakhedi is a medium-sized village of Sehore block, located 6 km. from Sehore town, on the Bhopal-Indore road. The village site is 1 km. away from the main road. With a population of 2200, most of the household are from *Khati Samaj,* a OBC community. *Khati* is also the dominant land-holding community. Nearly 45 household of the village were Scheduled Castes, who resided in separate settlement. Among SCs, *Balai* were in majority. In the land distribution programme *pattas* were allotted to 27 SC household in the entire *panchayat* area, however, similar to Satpiplya, as the encroachers on the *Charnoi* land were *Khaties* and the quality of land was good, SCs could not get any actual benefit due to the terror of the dominant and politically powerful *Khati Samaj* farmers.

7. Karohan

Karohan is a village of Ujjain block. To reach the village one has to travel 14 km. from Ujjain to Karohan fata, on Ujjain-Indore road and from this place a 7 km. branch road connects it to Karohan. The total population of the village was 1100. Out of 193 households *Patidar*, *Khati, Brahmin* and *Thakur* are the dominant castes and most of the agricultural land belong to them. Among SCs *Chamars, Balai* and *Mehtars* are the main castes who are largely agricultural labourers. The land quality in the village is very good. Out of 14 SCs who were allotted land two could not start cultivation because the allotted land was near a tank and was submerged under water at the time of survey.

8. Panthpiplya

Panthpiplya is a road side village, situated on the Ujjain–Indore road, 20 km. from Ujjain. Panthpiplya is a larger village with a population of 4000. It is a multi-caste village dominated by *Patidar, Yadav, Khati, Patel, Thakur* and *Brahmins*. First four, hailing from OBC, are the main land-holding castes. In the village all the 12 eligible allottees were allotted land. The quality of allotted land was good.

9. Sanodha

Sanodha is a large sized village of Sagar block and district. The village is located on Sagar–Damoh road, 22 km. from Sagar. The population of the village was 7835. It is a SC dominated village, and out of total 1455 households, 400 houses belonged to *Ahirwar* of SC category. However, *Thakur, Brahmin* and *Jains* control a major portion of agricultural land and are big farmers. The quality of agricultural land in the village is good. In the *panchayat area* 70 SC households were allotted *patta,* however, due to non- availability, all eligible persons could not be allotted land. The castes who were allotted land were *Ahirwar, Danak, Kotwar* and *Saur* from SC and *Gond* from ST.

10. Gidwani

Gidwani is a *panchayat* village of Sagar block and district. The village is well connected to Sagar. The population of the village was 1290. Out of the 239 households the majority belonged to *Lodhi* (100), *Dangi* (15), *Yadav* (18) and *Pal* (25) all were from OBC. These are also the main land holding castes in the village. The *sarpanch* of the village belonged to SC community. The soil of the village is medium to light black with abundant gravel. In the land distribution programme land was allotted to 16 families, 12 from SC and 4 from ST. Seven eligible families could not be allotted land mainly due to the inability of the administration to get the land freed from powerful encroachers.

11. Ghugra

Located in the forested tribal tract, the village Ghugra is located 18 km. from Mandla town, which is also the block and district headquarter. To reach the village one has to travel from Mandla to

Pedmi square, located on Jabalpur–Raipur highway. From Pedmi the village is 8 km. on a branch road. Direct bus connection to the village was also available from Mandla. The population of the village was 1240 with 275 households. In spite of being a tribal dominated area, the agricultural land was mainly controlled by *Brahmins* and *Lodhi*. The quality of soil is very good, however, the tribals generally owned fields having less fertile reddish soils. In the Ghugra *panchayat* 16 *pattas* were allotted in the land distribution programme, of which 13 were ST and 3 belonged to SC.

12. Hridaynagar

Hridaynagar panchayat village is located on Mandla–Bichiya road, 20 km. from Mandla town. The population of Hridaynagar was 3500. Out of 507 houses, around 300 belonged to tribals. Both the *sarpanch* and *patwari* were tribals. In spite of tribal dominance, non-tribals, namely, *Brahmin, Chourasia* and *Kushwah* control major portion of agricultural land. A majority of them are big farmers, with a land holding of 40 to 60 *bigha*. Scheduled Tribes are small farmers, owning 3 to 4 *bigha* and the land quality is also relatively inferior. During the land distribution programme land was allotted to 11 households, 10 of them were ST and 1 was SC.

13. Lalpur

Representing the eastern tribal belt, Lalpur village of Shahdol district is located on Shahdol–Budhar–Anuppur road, 17 km. from block headquarter Sohagpur. Being on National Highway No. 78, the village is well connected and is easily accessible. The village is a large village with a population of 5900. Out of the total household of 1188, the largest number of houses were of Scheduled Tribes. However, *Thakur, Sahu, Shukla* and *Garg Brahmin* control most of the agricultural land. Other castes include *Pal* and *Gaur*. Nearly all of the land which was distributed was already encroached land, being held by tribals. It was of inferior quality. Within *panchayat* a total of 24 *pattas* were distributed, 23 to ST and 1 to SC.

14. Kotma

Village Kotma is a tribal dominated village of Shahdol district. It is nearly 5 km. from Shahdol town and falls in Sohagpur block. Both the *sarpanch* and *patwari* belonged to Scheduled Tribes. The population of the village was 2100. Though *Gonds* are in majority, better class of land and big farms are controlled by *Brahmin*, *Jaiswal* and *Kachi* castes. The soil in the village is black–loamy. However, the agricultural land owned by the tribals is of inferior quality. Fourteen *pattas* were distributed in the land distribution programme and all of them were allottee those tribals who were already cultivating that land as encroachers.

15. Khunarjhiri

Khunarjhiri village is a medium-sized village of Mohankot block, district Chhindwada. The village is 14 km. from Chhindwada town and is located 3 km. from Imlikheda, on Chhindwara–Multai–Betul road. The village is well connected from Chhindwada and buses were available at frequent interval. The population of Khunarjhiri was 1550. Out of 249 households, the majority were tribals, however, *Kunbi, Gwali* and Muslims hold most of the agricultural land and are large farmers. The soil is mainly reddish loam, however, most of the agricultural land owned by tribals was stony. During land distribution programme 20 families were provided land in the *panchayat* and all of them were those tirbals who were in possession of that land as encroachers.

16. Mujawarmal

Mujawarmal is a big village of Chhindwada district with a population of 5000. It is directly connected to Chhindwada by a bus route, located nearly 10 km. from the town. The village falls in Mohankheda block. In spite of its being in tribal area, a major portion of good quality land is held by *Gawli, Panwar* and *Sahu,* all belonging to OBC. There were some houses of *Mehra* and *Chamars* who were from SC. The *Gonds* and *Mawasi* were the main tribal groups in the village. Nearly 40 per cent of agricultural land is very good quality black soil, 50 per cent is with gravel and 10 per cent is stony. All the allottees were tribals and were actually cultivating that land from years, though in record it was an unauthorized encroachment.

17. Beelpur

Beelpur is a village from Ambah block of Morena district. To reach the village one has first to travel by bus from Morena to Rajpur, located 23 km. from Morena on Morena–Ambah road and then a 12 km. branch road connects the village to Rajpur. The population of the village was 3000. Out of 600 household 400 houses were of *Thakurs,* 100 of *Baghel* (OBC) and 10 *Brahmins* who control most of the agricultural land. There were 25 SC families who were mostly agricultural labourers. The quality of agricultural land is very good. Within *panchayat* 31 *pattas* were allotted to *Chamars* and *Mehtars,* belonging to SC.

18. Joha

Joha is a panchayat village located 14 km. from Ranpur. Ranpur is situated on Morena–Ambah road. The population of the village was 1780. Out of approximately 300 households, 100 belonged to *Thakurs* and 125 were *Brahmins*. There were in all 39 houses of SC community who worked in the fields of *Thakurs* and *Brahmins*. In all 16 *pattas* were allotted, however, as the *patta* land was very uneven, most of them could not start cultivation in the absence of fund required for levelling the land.

Profile of Surveyed Household and Surveyed Population

As stated in table 3.1 a total of 279 household were surveyed in 18 sample village, out of which 150 belonged to Scheduled Castes and 129 were from Scheduled Tribes. The total population which was covered in the survey was 1658, out of which 899 were Scheduled Castes and the remaining 759 belonged to Scheduled Tribes category. The general profile of the surveyed household and surveyed population may be presented as follows :

Housing and Availability of Amenities

Conceding the fact that all the respondents belonged to the category of landless agricultural labourers, their economic condition was naturally poor. Their poor economic condition therefore, finds its expression both in the housing condition and the available amenities, as depicted in Table 3.2.

Table 3.2 shows that most of the houses of the respondents were either semi-*pucca* or *pucca,* only 16.1 per cent were *kaccha.*

Table 3.2 : House Type and Availability of Amenities to Surveyed Household

Village Code	District	Block	Sample Village	House Type %			Availability of amenities (% of total household)							
				Kaccha	*Pucca*	*Semi-pucca*	*Electricity*	*Piped Water at Home*	*Toilet at Residence*	*Bycycle*	*Radio/ Transistor*	*Motorcycle*	*Television*	*Fan*
1.	Dhar	Nalcha	Nai Baroda	50.0	10.0	40.0	35.0	-	10.0	20.0	15.0	5.0	20.0	15.0
2.	Dhar	Nalcha	Golarzhiri	36.8	21.1	42.1	47.4	5.3	31.6	36.8	36.8	10.5	21.1	21.1
3.	Hoshangabad	Bawai	Nagwada	13.3	53.3	33.4	100.0	-	-	20.0	6.7	-	13.3	13.3
4.	Hoshangabad	Bawai	Ganera	-	86.7	13.3	100.0	-	-	66.7	66.7	-	60.0	66.7
5.	Sehore	Sehore	Satpiplya	-	40.0	60.0	100.0	-	20.0	93.3	60.0	6.7	46.7	46.7
6.	Sehore	Sehore	Jattakhedi	13.3	13.3	73.4	100.0	-	-	80.0	60.0	-	40.0	40.0
7.	Ujjain	Ujjain	Karohan	20.0	20.0	60.0	100.0	-	13.3	73.3	66.4	-	20.0	20.0
8.	Ujjain	Ujjain	Panthpiplya	7.1	28.6	64.3	100.0	-	7.1	85.7	71.4	-	42.9	42.9
9.	Sagar	Sagar	Sanodha	-	93.3	6.6	100.0	-	-	53.3	46.7	-	-	-
10.	Sagar	Sagar	Gidwani	6.7	66.7	26.6	100.0	-	6.7	66.7	40.0	-	6.7	13.3
11.	Mandla	Mandla	Ghugra	-	20.0	80.0	53.3	-	6.7	53.3	53.3	-	20.0	13.3

(Contd.)

Table 3.2 *(Contd.)*

Village Code	*District*	*Block*	*Sample Village*	*House Type %*			*Availability of amenities (% of total household)*							
				Kaccha	*Pucca*	*Semi-pucca*	*Electricity*	*Piped Water at Home*	*Toilet at Residence*	*Bycycle*	*Radio/ Transistor*	*Motorcycle*	*Television*	*Fan*
12.	Mandla	Mandla	Hridaynagar	13.3	33.3	53.4	53.3	20.0	6.7	20.0	53.3	-	13.3	20.0
13.	Shehdol	Suhagpur	Lalpur	13.3	-	86.7	NIL	-	6.7	80.0	80.0	6.6	-	-
14.	Shehdol	Suhagpur	Kotma	6.7	26.7	66.6	6.7	-	6.7	40.0	33.3	-	-	-
15.	Chhindwada	Chhindwada	Khunarjhiri	13.3	46.7	40.0	93.3	-	-	73.3	53.3	-	6.7	20.0
16.	Chhindwada	Chhindwada	Mujawarmal	6.7	66.7	26.6	80.0	-	-	73.3	13.3	-	6.7	6.7
17.	Morena	Ambah	Beelpur	73.3	6.7	20.0	NIL	6.7	6.7	73.3	6.7	-	-	-
18.	Morena	Ambah	Joha	-	60.0	40.0	80.0	-	-	93.3	40.0	-	33.3	26.7
Total SC				13.3	46.7	40.0	87.3	0.7	5.3	70.7	46.7	0.7	26.7	27.3
Total ST				19.4	27.1	53.5	45.7	3.1	9.3	48.8	41.1	3.1	11.6	12.4
Grand Total				16.1	37.6	46.3	68.1	1.8	7.2	60.6	44.1	1.8	19.7	20.4

Relatively Scheduled Castes were having higher percentage of *pucca* houses, as compared to tribals. Tribals, especially of forest areas, prefer to built log houses with tiled roofs that are classed as semi-*pucca*. Wide variation was also apparent within villages, for example, in village Sanodha and Gidwani of Sagar district a majority of houses were *pucca*, while this percentage was very low in Beelpur and Nai Baroda. In the village Lalpur of Shehdol none of the respondents was having a *pucca* house.

Due to physical isolation of the dwellings the electric connection in tribal huts was found to be only 45.7 per cent, as compared to 87.3 per cent in SC houses. Most of the connections were one point, provided by the government a highly subsidized cost. Both the piped water or toilet facility within the dwellings was available to only few, and that too was in few villages. Nearly 71 per cent of the SC household possessed bicycle, while only 49 per cent of the tribal household were having a bicycle, mainly due to the reason that it was not useful in rugged terrain. Nearly 44 per cent of household possessed a transistor, and on this count there was no significant difference between SCs and STs. Due to lower availability of electricity only 11.6 per cent of the ST household were possessing TV sets, while this percentage was 26.7 in the case of SCs. Similarly the ownership of fan with STs was less than half than their SC counterpart. Motorcycle was being possessed by only few person in villages like Golarzhiri, Satpiplya and Lalpur.

Age, Sex and Literacy Level of Studied Population

The sex ratio of the sample population was 1001, showing thereby a perfect balanced condition. Within the sample the sex ratio of ST and SC population was respectively 1031 and 979, showing a higher male selectivity amongst the SCs. The sample depicted a younger population, in that, nearly 38 per cent of the total population was represented by children below 14 years of age. A significantly larger percentage of child population is an indicator of a situation in which the number of job seekers will be quite large in future, as compared to agricultural assets available at present and are being provided to the family under the programme.

The literacy level of the surveyed population was 33.1 per cent, which was more or less similar for both the SCs and STs. As

Table 3.3 : Age Sex and Literacy Level of Surveyed Population

Village Code	*District*	*Block*	*Sample Village*	*Total Surveyed Population*	*Male Above 14 Years*	*Female Above 14 Years*	*Children Below 14 Years*	*Literates (% of Total Surveyed Population)*	*Persons High School and Above (% of Persons Above 14)*
1.	Dhar	Nalcha	Nai Baroda	106	30	26	50	44.3	3.6
2.	Dhar	Nalcha	Golarzhiri	122	33	42	47	35.2	Nil
3.	Hoshangabad	Bawai	Nagwada	84	30	27	27	39.3	5.3
4.	Hoshangabad	Bawai	Ganera	77	30	26	21	36.4	3.6
5.	Sehore	Sehore	Satpiplya	85	21	28	36	43.5	6.1
6.	Sehore	Sehore	Jattakhedi	88	26	31	31	28.4	3.5
7.	Ujjain	Ujjain	Karohan	70	21	25	24	27.1	4.3
8.	Ujjain	Ujjain	Panthpiplya	91	24	32	35	27.6	Nil
9.	Sagar	Sagar	Sanodha	89	35	26	28	52.8	8.2
10.	Sagar	Sagar	Gidwani	90	29	24	37	47.8	5.7
11.	Mandla	Mandla	Ghugra	81	24	25	32	43.2	2

(Contd.)

Table 3.3 *(Contd.)*

Village Code	*District*	*Block*	*Sample Village*	*Total Surveyed Population*	*Male Above 14 Years*	*Female Above 14 Years*	*Children Below 14 Years*	*Literates (% of Total Surveyed Population)*	*Persons High School and Above (% of Persons Above 14)*
12.	Mandla	Mandla	Hridaynagar	64	20	21	23	43.8	7.3
13.	Shehdol	Suhagpur	Lalpur	109	40	35	34	27.5	Nil
14.	Shehdol	Suhagpur	Kotma	90	29	32	29	12.2	Nil
15.	Chhindwada	Chhindwada	Khunarjhiri	93	26	30	37	31.2	5.4
16.	Chhindwada	Chhindwada	Mujawarmal	94	25	23	46	9.6	Nil
17.	Morena	Ambah	Beelpur	125	45	37	43	28	9.8
18.	Morena	Ambah	Joha	100	28	27	45	25	5.5
		Total SC		899	289	283	327	35.3	5.4
		Total ST		759	227	234	298	30.6	2.0
		Grand Total		1658	516	517	625	33.1	3.9

far as the percentage of persons who were high school or above, it was very low; 2.0 per cent for SCs and 5.4 per cent for STs.

Work Status

As the sample consisted of agricultural labourers, the work participation (among above 14 year age group) was much higher at 80.9 per cent, as compared to average provincial value of 42.7, as per 2001 Census. It was even higher in STs (85.2%) than among SCs (77.4%). The work participation was high consistently in all the sample villages and most of the dependents were either too old to work or were below 14 years of age.

Among tribal surveyed population, dependence on agricultural labour for livelihood was as high as 96.7 per cent, while amongst SCs the percentage was 81.9. However, this difference was caused due to the inclusion of the villages of Sagar district where *bidi* making was an important economic activity. The level of skill was found to be extremely low at 1.3 per cent and the contribution of tertiary sector, viz. service or trade and commerce was also not significant and was restricted only to few individuals.

IV

Research Questions

As per the laid down objectives, in the following analysis an attempt has been made to evaluate the following, based on the survey conducted in the sample villages:

(i) Whether those who were allotted the *patta* were genuine ones and could actually hold the land ?

(ii) What was the status of ownership, previous and present?

(iii) What had been the size of *patta*, quality of land and access to productive resources.

(iv) Evaluation of the net financial benefits accrued to the allotteess, and

(v) Perceived enhancement of status.

Allotment of *Patta*

As per the guideline the allotment had to be made only to persons belonging to Scheduled Castes and Scheduled Tribes, firstly, to

Table 3.4 : Work Status of Surveyed Population

Village Code	*District*	*Block*	*Sample Village*	*Gainful Workers (% of Persons Above 14 Years of Age)*	*Dependents (% Of total Surveyed Population)*	*Type of Work (% of Worker)*				
						Agriculture Plus Unskilled Labour	*Skilled Workers Mechanic, Mason, etc.)*	*In Service*	*Trade and Commerce*	*Other : Bidi Making, Midwife etc.*
1.	Dhar	Nalcha	Nai Baroda	94.6	50.0	92.4	-	3.8	-	3.8
2.	Dhar	Nalcha	Golarzhiri	73.3	54.9	89.2	7.2	3.6	-	-
3.	Hoshangabad	Bawai	Nagwada	78.9	46.4	100.0	-	-	-	-
4.	Hoshangabad	Bawai	Ganera	73.2	46.8	97.6	-	-	2.4	-
5.	Sehore	Sehore	Satpiplya	75.5	56.5	91.9	-	-	-	8.1
6.	Sehore	Sehore	Jattakhedi	77.2	50.0	93.2	-	-	6.8	-
7.	Ujjain	Ujjain	Karohan	82.6	45.7	86.8	-	5.3	7.9	-
8.	Ujjain	Ujjain	Panthpiplya	71.7	56.3	87.1	2.6	-	10	-
9.	Sagar	Sagar	Sanodha	85.2	41.6	69.2	-	-	-	30.8
10.	Sagar	Sagar	Gidwani	96.2	44.4	64.7	3.9	-	-	31.4
11.	Mandla	Mandla	Ghugra	85.7	48.1	100.0	-	-	-	-

(Contd.)

Table 3.4 *(Contd.)*

Village Code	*District*	*Block*	*Sample Village*	*Gainful Workers (% of Persons Above 14 Years of Age)*	*Dependents (% Of total Surveyed Population)*	*Type of Work (% of Worker)*				
						Agriculture Plus Unskilled Labour	*Skilled Workers Mechanic, Mason, etc.)*	*In Service*	*Trade and Commerce*	*Other : Bidi Making, Midwife etc.*
12.	Mandla	Mandla	Hridaynagar	87.8	43.8	94.4	2.8	-	-	2.8
13.	Shehdol	Suhagpur	Lalpur	81.3	44.0	98.3	-	1.7	-	-
14.	Shehdol	Suhagpur	Kotma	93.4	36.7	100.0	-	-	-	-
15.	Chhindwada	Chhindwada	Khunarjhiri	83.9	49.5	100.0	-	-	-	-
16.	Chhindwada	Chhindwada	Mujawarmal	87.5	55.3	100.0	-	-	-	-
17.	Morena	Ambah	Beelpur	63.4	58.4	78.8	-	1.9	-	19.3
18.	Morena	Ambah	Joha	80.0	56.0	65.9	-	9.1	-	25
		Total SC		77.4	50.7	81.9	1.4	2.3	1.8	12.6
		Total ST		85.2	48.2	96.7	1.3	1.3	-	0.7
		Grand Total		80.9	49.6	88.9	1.3	1.8	1.0	7.0

landless persons of category I and then to category II. On this count no discrepancy was observed in the survey. No case was reported where allotment may have been made to other than SC or ST, or the preferential order for category I and II may not have been maintained. However, in one sample village, namely, Beelpur of Morena district it was informed by the people that in some cases three to four *pattas* were given to persons within one family only, defying the definition of a landless family.

In the programme it was basically conceived that prior to allotment all the government grazing land which was declared surplus, after reducing the percentage from 5 to 2, would be marked and freed from all encroachments. In most of the tribal villages where encroachers were tribals, barring few cases reported in villages Lalpur (Shehdol), Khunarjhiri (Chhindwada) and Mujarwarmal (Chhindwada) where some of the tribal encroachers could not be given legal entitlement, in most of the cases either the same encroacher was given the legal entitlement, or if the size of land encroached was more than 2 hectares, the surplus was allotted to some other tribal, preferably to his near relative. However, most of the violations were reported in villages where the encroachers were from non-SC, ST category. During group discussion held in the sample villages, in 9 out of 18 villages it was reported that some influential persons from other communities were still holding the government land and their encroachment was either not reported by *patwari*, or due to their political alignment, no serious attempt was made to free that land for distribution. In stead some poor quality piece of government land was allotted to them. For example, in Genera (Hoshangabad) and Joha (Morena) in some cases the allotted land was so much uneven that the allotteess had no resources to level that land, and therefore, could not start cultivation. A queer case was reported in the village Beelpur (Morena) where the encroachers was *Thakurs* who were cultivating government land since last 15-20 years and they had constructed wells and done contour bunding on that land. Though this fertile land was officially got released and distributed to SCs, the allottees, realising the fact that it would not be possible for them to stand against *Thakurs* and cultivate that land, it was unofficially transferred to them on plain paper, after receiving a cash of Rs. 10 to 15 thousand per bigha. Thus, on record the land distribution programme was accomplished successfully without any conflict, in reality they were still workers on *Thakurs* fields, though they could earn some cash which was less than half the existing market price.

The information pertaining to the allotment of *pattas* to the surveyed household has been tabulated in Table 3.5.

Table 3.5 clarifies that in a majority of cases the allottees were actually holding the land. The position was quite positive with respect to ST household where 96.1 per cent of the allottees were found to actually hold the land. This situation was apparent because most of these farmers were cultivating this land prior to the legal allotment. The allottees who were not legally holding the land among STs were either due to delay in process or their land was submerged under the tank (Nai Baroda) at the time of allotment. No deleberate attemp of not allowing them to hold and cultivate the allotted land was reported with respect to ST respondents. The situation was, however, different in the case of SC allottees, especially when the actual encroachers were from non-SC/ST category and the quality of land was good. Special mention may be made regarding Jattakhedi and Panthpiplya villages of Sehore district where the land quality was good and the actual encroachers were economically and politically powerful *Khati* community. In Jattakhedi the *Khaties* did not allow 80 per cent allottees to cultivate the land, the SCs were also hesitant to apply force as they were under a threat of stoppage of work on *Khaties* field. In Panthpiplya where in a serious conflict one SC died and the entire administration was mobilized, although all the allottees were allotteed land on paper, the allottees of *Basod* community who received financial gratification for midwife work, in a fear of loosing their traditional job, did not cultivate the field and unofficially let the *Khaties* cultivate their land as before.

In the village Ganera (Hoshangabad) nearly 13 per cent of the SC allottees could not cultivate the land because the allotted land was uneven and they did not have the funds to level the land. In the village of Beelpur (Morena) as described previously, though the allottees were holding the land on paper, unofficially a large number of them had unofficially sold that land to *Thakurs* for 15 to 20 thousand rupees per bigha. In the village Joha (Morena) two-third

Table 3.5 : Information About the Allotment of *Patta* to the Surveyed Household

Village Code	*District*	*Block*	*Sample Village*	*Whether Actually Holding (% of Household)*	*Status of Cultivation (% of Actual Holding)*			*Ownership Category (% of Allottees)*		
					Self	*Given or Sold to Other*	*Not Cultivating*	*To Male Member*	*To Female Member*	*Joint Ownership*
1.	Dhar	Nalcha	Golarzhiri	100.0	100.0	-	-	80.0	20.0	-
2.	Dhar	Nalcha	Nai Baroda	84.2	100.0	-	-	56.3	43.7	-
3.	Hoshangabad	Bawai	Ganera	93.3	71.4	-	28.6	-	-	100.0
4.	Hoshangabad	Bawai	Nangwada	66.7	100.0	-	-	66.6	-	33.4
5.	Sehore	Sehore	Satpiplya	100.0	80.0	-	20.0	-	20.0	80.0
6.	Sehore	Sehore	Jattakhedi	20.0	100.0	-	-	-	-	100.0
7.	Ujjain	Ujjain	Karohan	100.0	100.0	-	-	86.7	13.3	-
8.	Ujjain	Ujjain	Panthpipliya	100.0	100.0	-	-	28.6	50.0	214.0
9.	Sagar	Sagar	Sanodha	100.0	100.0	-	-	13.3	13.3	73.4
10.	Sagar	Sagar	Gidwani	100.0	100.0	-	-	26.7	6.7	66.6
11.	Mandla	Mandla	Ghughra	100.0	53.3	46.7	-	53.3	26.7	20.0

(Contd.)

Table 3.5 *(Contd.)*

Village Code	*District*	*Block*	*Sample Village*	*Whether Actually Holding (% of Household)*	*Status of Cultivation (% of Actual Holding)*			*Ownership Category (% of Allottees)*		
					Self	*Given or Sold to Other*	*Not Cultivating*	*To Male Member*	*To Female Member*	*Joint Ownership*
12.	Mandla	Mandla	Haridaynagar	86.7	76.9	-	23.1	86.8	6.6	6.6
13.	Shehdol	Suhagpur	Lalpur	100.0	100.0	-	-	93.3	6.7	-
14.	Shehdol	Suhagpur	Kotma	100.0	100.0	-	-	100.0	-	-
15.	Chhindwada	Chhindwada	Khunarzhiri	100.0	100.0	-	-	73.3	26.7	-
16.	Chhindwada	Chhindwada	Mujawarmal	100.0	100.0	-	-	100.0	-	-
17.	Morena	Ambah	Bilpur	93.3	100.0	-	-	13.3	20.0	66.7
18.	Morena	Ambah	Joha	33.3	100.0	-	-	-	-	100.0
			Total SC	80.7	94.2	-	5.8	24.0	12.0	64.0
			Total ST	96.1	91.9	5.6	2.5	80.6	16.3	3.1
			Grand Total	87.8	93.1	2.9	4.0	50.2	14.0	35.8

of the allottees refused to occupy the allotteed land due to poor quality and requirement of heavy investment for making it cultivable.

In nearly all cases the ST farmers who were allotted land were cultivating the land. Only in villages Ghughra and Hridaynagar of Mandla district some farmers had not started growing crops mostly because the land was made available very recently. In few cases the *Kathies* were creating problems and were not allowing the tribals to start growing crops.

Status of Ownership, Previous and Present

As clarified earlier most of the so called *Charnoi* land which was classed as government land and was distributed under land distribution programme was under unauthorized occupation. These encroachers were paying some fine and were continuing their control on this land. In the sample villages also, out of a total allotment of 279 *pattas,* only 71, i.e., 25.4 per cent of it was vacant land which was in government possession. In 40.5 per cent of the cases the allottees were the original encroachers while in the remaining 59.5 the previous owners were different than the encroachers. A marked difference was noted among the SC and ST sample. While in the ST villages 77.5 per cent allottees were the original encroachers and only 22.5 per cent were those who received the *patta* not previously held by them. This percentage was respectively 8.7 and 91.3 per cent in the case of Scheduled Castes allottees, meaning thereby that a very high percentage among SC allottees were those who were allotted land that was previously held by someone, other than themselves.

The villagewise information relating to those allottees who were previously cultivating the same land as encroachers and those who received a fresh allotment has respectively been tabulated in Tables 3.6 and 3.7.

Table 3.6 clarifies that in most of the tribal villages the allotment was made to those who were previously cultivating that land. Among these allottees half of them had to part away with some of their encroached land because the encroachment was more than the specified limit of 2 hectares. During survey it was revealed that the allotment of surplus encroachment land was mostly made to their near relatives to avoid conflicts, and therefore, the conflicts

Table 3.6 : Allottees who were Previously Cultivating the Allotted Land

Village Code	*District*	*Block*	*Sample Village*	*Allottees who were Previously Cultivating the Land allotted to them (% of Allottees)*	*Allottees who had to Part with Some of Their Encroachment (% of Allottees who were Themselves Cultivating)*	*Disputes in Giving away that Land (% of Cases)*
1.	Dhar	Nalcha	Nai Baroda	100.0	-	-
2.	Dhar	Nalcha	Golarzhiri	81.3	18.7	100.0
3.	Hoshangabad	Bawai	Nagwada	20.0	100.0	-
4.	Hoshangabad	Bawai	Ganera	Nil	NA	NA
5.	Sehore	Sehore	Satpiplya	Nil	NA	NA
6.	Sehore	Sehore	Jattakhedi	Nil	NA	NA
7.	Ujjain	Ujjain	Karohan	66.7	66.7	6.7
8.	Ujjain	Ujjain	Panthpiplya	Nil	NA	NA
9.	Sagar	Sagar	Sanodha	Nil	NA	NA
10.	Sagar	Sagar	Gidwani	Nil	NA	NA
11.	Mandla	Mandla	Ghugra	20.0	33.3	33.3

(Contd.)

Table 3.6 *(Contd.)*

Village Code	*District*	*Block*	*Sample Village*	*Allottees who were Previously Cultivating the Land allotted to them (% of Allottees)*	*Allottees who had to Part with Some of Their Encroachment (% of Allottees who were Themselves Cultivating)*	*Disputes in Giving away that Land (% of Cases)*
12.	Mandla	Mandla	Hridaynagar	6.6	100.0	-
13.	Shehdol	Suhagpur	Lalpur	100.0	NIL	Nil
14.	Shehdol	Suhagpur	Kotma	100.0	100.0	Nil
15.	Chhindwada	Chhindwada	Khunarjhiri	100.0	100.0	Nil
16.	Chhindwada	Chhindwada	Mujawarmal	100.0	100.0	Nil
17.	Morena	Ambah	Beelpur	Nil	NA	NA
18.	Morena	Ambah	Joha	Nil	NA	NA
			Total SC	8.7	100.0	7.7
			Total ST	77.5	50.0	8.0
			Grand Total	40.5	55.8	7.9

Table 3.7 : Allottees who were Allotted Land not Previously Held by Them

Village Code	*District*	*Block*	*Sample Village*	*Allottes whose Allotteed Land was Previously Held by Some one else (% of Allottes)*	*Category of Previous Encroacher (%)*				
					General	*Scheduled Castes*	*Scheduled Tribes*	*Other Backward Classes*	*Vacant Government Land*
1.	Dhar	Nalcha	Nai Baroda	-	NA	NA	NA	NA	NA
2.	Dhar	Nalcha	Golarzhiri	18.7	100.0	-	-	-	-
3.	Hoshangabad	Bawai	Nagwada	80.0	-	-	-	91.7	8.3
4.	Hoshangabad	Bawai	Ganera	100.0	6.7	-	-	33.3	60.0
5.	Sehore	Sehore	Satpiplya	100.0	-	-	-	100.0	-
6.	Sehore	Sehore	Jattakhedi	100.0	-	-	-	100.0	-
7.	Ujjain	Ujjain	Karohan	33.3	-	-	-	100.0	-
8.	Ujjain	Ujjain	Panthpiplya	100.0	7.1	7.1	-	7.1	78.7
9.	Sagar	Sagar	Sanodha	100.0	-	-	-	-	100.0
10.	Sagar	Sagar	Gidwani	100.0	-	20.0	-	-	80.0
11.	Mandla	Mandla	Ghugra	80.0	-	-	66.7	33.3	-

(Contd.)

Table 3.7 *(Contd.)*

Village Code	*District*	*Block*	*Sample Village*	*Allottes whose Allotted Land was Previously Held by Some one else (% of Allottes)*	*Category of Previous Encroacher (%)*				
					General	*Scheduled Castes*	*Scheduled Tribes*	*Other Backward Classes*	*Vacant Government Land*
12.	Mandla	Mandla	Hridaynagar	93.3	7.1	-	-	14.3	78.6
13.	Shehdol	Suhagpur	Lalpur	Nil	NA	-	-	-	-
14.	Shehdol	Suhagpur	Kotma	Nil	NA	-	-	-	-
15.	Chhindwada	Chhindwada	Khunarjhiri	Nil	NA	-	-	-	-
16.	Chhindwada	Chhindwada	Mujawarmal	Nil	NA	-	-	-	-
17.	Morena	Ambah	Beelpur	100.0	100.0	-	-	-	-
18.	Morena	Ambah	Joha	100.0	60.0	-	-	-	40.0
			Total SC	91.3	19.0	2.9	-	34.3	43.8
			Total ST	22.5	13.8	-	27.6	20.7	37.9
			Grand Total	59.5	18.0	2.4	4.8	31.9	42.9

were reported in less than 10 per cent of the cases. However, the parting away with some of the land resulted in strained relations among relatives and the entire process was perceived as a process which created rift among people of the same caste.

In the case of Scheduled Castes 91.3 per cent of them received fresh *patta*, i.e., they were not cultivating the land previously. Out of these allottees 43.8 per cent got the *patta* on vacant government land and in most of the cases this land was of poor quality. Out of the remaining 56.2 per cent land, 19.0 per cent was got released from general castes persons, 2.9 per cent from SC and 34.3 per cent from OBC. In the sample villages of Satpiplya, Jattakhedi (Sehore) and Karohan (Ujjain) the entire government land had been encroached by powerful OBC and these were the cases where stiff resistance was created by the powerful land-owning castes and various cases of conflicts were reported. Sanodha (Sagar) was an exception where the entire land that was distributed, was vacant government land.

In the case of Scheduled Tribes only 22.5 per cent received the land which was not held previously by them. Out of this land 37.9 per cent was vacant government land and 27.6 per cent was got released from ST where no disputes were reported. Nai Baroda (Dhar) was the only surveyed tribal village where the encroachers were from upper castes while in Mandla some of the land was got released from OBC farmers.

Land Quality, Size of *Patta,* and Access of Productive Resources

The quality and fertility status of the allotted land has been depicted in Table 3.8. The table shows that, on an average nearly 55 per cent of the allotted *pattas* were on level land. However, a marked difference was noted between the surveyed SC and ST household. In the case of tribal allottees 64.3 per cent *pattas* were on slopping land, while for SCs 72.3 per cent were level fields. Within villages also a large variation was found in the degree of levelness of the allotted land. While in Nai Baroda (Dhar), Nagwada (Hoshangabad), Ganera (Hoshangabad), Ghugra (Mandla), Hridaynagar (Mandla), and Mujawarmal (Chhindwada) 73 to 93 per cent of the allotted *pattas* were on slopping land, in Joha (Morena), Beelpur (Morena), Gidwani (Sagar), Sanodha (Sagar),

Table 3.8 : Land Quality and Fertility Level of the Allotted Land

Village Code	*District*	*Block*	*Sample Village*	*Degree of Levelness (% of Allottees)*			*Fertility Level (% of Allottees)*				
				Sloping	*Level Field*	*In Depression*	*Stoney*	*Gravelly*	*Unproductive*	*Average Quality*	*Fertile*
1.	Dhar	Nalcha	Nai Baroda	85.0	15.0	-	50.0	45.0	-	5.0	-
2.	Dhar	Nalcha	Golarzhiri	56.3	43.7	-	42.1	10.5	-	47.4	-
3.	Hoshangabad	Bawai	Nagwada	86.7	13.3	-	6.7	66.6	6.7	6.7	13.3
4.	Hoshangabad	Bawai	Ganera	86.7	13.3	-	-	53.3	13.3	6.7	26.7
5.	Sehore	Sehore	Satpiplya	-	100.0	-	-	-	-	-	100.0
6.	Sehore	Sehore	Jattakhedi	26.7	66.7	6.6	-	-	6.7	40.0	53.3
7.	Ujjain	Ujjain	Karohan	6.6	93.4	-	6.7	6.7	-	20.0	66.6
8.	Ujjain	Ujjain	Panthpiplya	35.7	64.3	-	-	-	-	57.1	42.9
9.	Sagar	Sagar	Sanodha	6.7	93.3	-	40.0	60.0	-	-	-
10.	Sagar	Sagar	Gidwani	6.7	93.3	-	6.7	40.0	20.0	33.3	-
11.	Mandla	Mandla	Ghugra	80.0	20.0	-	-	-	33.3	13.3	53.4

(Contd.)

Table 3.8 *(Contd.)*

Village Code	District	Block	Sample Village	Degree of Levelness (% of Allottees)			Fertility Level (% of Allottees)				
				Sloping	Level Field	In Depression	Stoney	Gravelly	Unproductive	Average Quality	Fertile
12.	Mandla	Mandla	Hridaynagar	93.3	6.7	-	6.7	6.7	20.0	46.6	20.0
13.	Shehdol	Suhagpur	Lalpur	66.7	33.3	-	40.0	-	-	40.0	20.0
14.	Shehdol	Suhagpur	Kotma	26.7	73.3	-	-	20.0	-	73.3	6.7
15.	Chhindwada	Chhindwada	Khunarjhiri	33.3	66.7	-	6.7	33.3	-	40.0	20.20
16.	Chhindwada	Chhindwada	Mujawarmal	73.3	26.7	-	60.0	13.3	-	26.7	-
17.	Morena	Ambah	Beelpur	-	93.3	6.7	-	-	6.7	6.7	86.6
18.	Morena	Ambah	Joha	-	93.3	6.7	-	33.3	6.7	60.0	-
			Total SC	26.0	72.0	2.0	6.0	26.0	6.0	23.3	38.7
			Total ST	64.3	35.7	-	27.1	17.1	6.2	35.6	14.0
			Grand Total	43.7	55.2	1.1	15.8	21.9	6.1	29.0	27.2

Karohan (Ujjain), and Satpiplya (Sehore) more than 90 per cent of the allotted *pattas* were on level land.

As far as the fertility level was concerned, a marked difference was noted between SC and ST allottees. In SC sample 38.7 per cent was stated to be of good quality and 23.3 per cent of average quality, while in the case of ST sample only 14.0 per cent was rated to be of good quality and 35.6 per cent of average quality. Due to hilly location of tribal villages 27.1 per cent of the allotted land was stony in nature while this percentage was only 6.0 in the case of SC household. A marked inter village contrast in the fertility level was also noted. While, on the one hand in Satpiplya (Sehore) and Beelpur (Morena) villages respectively 100 per cent and 86.6 per cent of allotted fields were rated as fertile land, in Nai Baroda (Dhar), Golarzhiri (Dhar), Sanodha (Sagar), Gidwani (Sagar), Mujawarmal (Chhindwada) and Joha (Morena) none of the allotted *pattas* were rated to be as fertile.

The size of *pattas* allotted has been shown in Table 3.9. The average size of *patta* worked out to be 0.97 hectare, however, there was a marked difference between the SC and ST allottees. The average size was 1.25 hectare for the SC sample, as compared to 0.65 hectare for the tribal allottees. As per the guideline no one was to be allotted land below 0.5 hectare, however, there had been a violation, especially in tribal villages, where 27.1 per cent of the *pattas* were of below 0.5 hectare in size. In villages Panthapiplya (Ujjain), Ghugra (Mandla), Hridaynagar (Mandla) and Kotma (Shehdol) a large number of *pattas* were found to be of very small in size.

The accessibility of the allotted land was found to be difficult, especially in those villages where the original encroachers were from powerful non SC/ST category. For example in Satpiplya and Jattakhedi villages conditions were deliberately created so that the SCs may not be able to enter their fields and sow crops. In tribal sample villages of Mandla district also some cases were reported where the access to actual allottees was difficult due to their vulnerable position. However, in general the problem of access was relatively much less in tribal villages.

Table 3.9 : Size of Land, Availability of Irrigation and Access

Village Code	*District*	*Block*	*Sample Village*	*Patta Allotted per Household (in Hectares)*	Size of *Patta*			*Availability of irrigation (% of Allottees)*	*Difficult Access (% of Allottees)*
					0 to 0.5 hect. (% of Allottees)	*0.5 to 1.0 hect.*	*1.0 hect. and Above*		
1.	Dhar	Nalcha	Nai Baroda	1.0	-	-	100.0	10.0	-
2.	Dhar	Nalcha	Golarzhiri	1.0	-	-	100.0	31.3	18.7
3.	Hoshangabad	Bawai	Nagwada	1.09	-	33.3	66.7	20.0	6.7
4.	Hoshangabad	Bawai	Ganera	0.85	-	60.0	40.0	Nil	40.0
5.	Sehore	Sehore	Satpiplya	1.59	-	-	100.0	Nil	86.7
6.	Sehore	Sehore	Jattakhedi	1.39	-	46.7	53.3	Nil	86.7
7.	Ujjain	Ujjain	Karohan	0.45	20.0	80.0	-	13.3	13.3
8.	Ujjain	Ujjain	Panthpiplya	0.40	57.1	42.9	-	-	14.2
9.	Sagar	Sagar	Sanodha	0.7	-	100.0	-	Nil	Nil
10.	Sagar	Sagar	Gidwani	0.86	6.7	60.0	33.3	Nil	Nil
11.	Mandla	Mandla	Ghugra	0.26	66.6	33.4	-	-	20.0

(Contd.)

Table 3.9 *(Contd.)*

Village Code	*District*	*Block*	*Sample Village*	*Patta Allotted per Household (in Hectares)*	Size of *Patta*			*Availability of irrigation (% of Allottees)*	*Difficult Access (% of Allottees)*
					0 to 0.5 hect. (% of Allottees)	*0.5 to 1.0 hect.*	*1.0 hect. and Above*		
12.	Mandla	Mandla	Hridaynagar	0.35	93.3	6.7	-	6.7	13.3
13.	Shehdol	Suhagpur	Lalpur	0.74	-	86.7	13.3	-	Nil
14.	Shehdol	Suhagpur	Kotma	0.39	60.0	40.0	-	-	6.7
15.	Chhindwada	Chhindwada	Khunarjhiri	0.77	6.7	60.0	33.3	53.3	Nil
16.	Chhindwada	Chhindwada	Mujawarmal	0.66	6.7	73.3	20.0	6.7	Nil
17.	Morena	Ambah	Beelpur	3.08	-	-	100.0	6.7	Nil
18.	Morena	Ambah	Joha	2.1	-	-	100.0	-	26.7
			Total SC	1.25	8.7	42.0	49.3	4.0	27.3
			Total ST	0.65	27.1	34.9	38.0	13.2	7.0
			Grand Total	0.97	17.2	38.7	44.1	8.2	17.9

As per Table 3.9 availability of irrigation was found to be generally low, however, it varied from individual to individual. On those fields which were under encroachment by the same farmer for long period, irrigation facility had been created by them. Such cases were found in the villages like Khunarjhiri (Chhindwada), Nagwada (Hoshangabad) and Golarjhiri (Dhar).

The Financial Benefit

A rough estimate of the investment made and output from the allotted land was made for all the respondents pertaining to two agricultural seasons, i.e., *rabi* and *kharif* of the previous year. The items which were included for making this estimate are as follows:

A. Expenditure

1. For the acquisition of *patta.*
2. Cost of production, *rabi* and *kharif*
   - (i) Levelling of land
   - (ii) Fertilizer purchased
   - (iii) Seed
   - (iv) Insecticide/pesticide
   - (v) Rent for irrigation, equipment, transport etc.
   - (vi) Paid up labour cost
   - (vii) Loss of wages.

B. Income

Quantity of crops produced in *rabi* and *kharif*, multiplied by market value.

The computation of income and expenditure for each sample village and for the entire sample, both with respect to SC and ST respondents, has been presented in Table 3.10.

A casual look at Table 3.10 brings out that, barring few exceptions, the allottees had not to spend money, as bribe or gratification, for acquiring the *patta*. However, during group discussion it came to light that many powerful farmers who had encroachment on good quality government land were still holding their encroachment by hook or crook and thus, some other poor quality land was shown as surplus and was distributed. Many allottees who paid money to *patwari* were also reluctant to give this information. A general feeling among the villagers was that

Table 3.10 : Expenditure and Income from (Rupees per hectare)

Village Code	*District*	*Block*	*Sample Village*	*Expenditure in Acquiring Patta (Rupees per hectare)*	*Average Annual Paid up Cost (in Rupees per Household)*	*Average Gross Annual Income (Rupees per Household)*	*Average Net Income per Household (in Rupees)*
1.	Dhar	Nalcha	Nai Baroda	136	2043	6520	4477
2.	Dhar	Nalcha	Golarzhiri	100	2122	6593	4471
3.	Hoshangabad	Bawai	Nagwada	Nil	928	3129	2201
4.	Hoshangabad	Bawai	Ganera	-	1670	5890	4220
5.	Sehore	Sehore	Satpiplya	-	2333	13847	11514
6.	Sehore	Sehore	Jattakhedi	1677	2800	13167	10166
7.	Ujjain	Ujjain	Karohan	-	2067	5203	3136
8.	Ujjain	Ujjain	Panthpiplya	-	1389	4535	3146
9.	Sagar	Sagar	Sanodha	371	1965	1413	(-) 552
10.	Sagar	Sagar	Gidwani	151	1483	2801	1318
11.	Mandla	Mandla	Ghugra	77	-	807	807

(Contd.)

Table 3.10 *(Contd.)*

Village Code	*District*	*Block*	*Sample Village*	*Expenditure in Acquiring Patta (Rupees per hectare)*	*Average Annual Paid up Cost (in Rupees per Household)*	*Average Gross Annual Income (Rupees per Household)*	*Average Net Income per Household (in Rupees)*
12.	Mandla	Mandla	Hridaynagar	-	23	1257	1234
13.	Shehdol	Suhagpur	Lalpur	-	187	2536	2349
14.	Shehdol	Suhagpur	Kotma	20	40	1927	1887
15.	Chhindwada	Chhindwada	Khunarjhiri	33	1020	6263	5243
16.	Chhindwada	Chhindwada	Mujawarmal	-	1360	6553	5193
17.	Morena	Ambah	Beelpur	-	1421	15564	14143
18.	Morena	Ambah	Joha	40	880	5660	4780
			Total SC	208	1759	7046	5287
			Total ST	65	1001	4592	3591
			Grand Total	164	1284	5415	4131

the entire programme of land distribution provided good opportunity for local level officials to make money.

The overall annual net financial gain worked out to Rs. 4131 per household, without taking into account their own labour cost. The gain was significantly higher for SC respondents at Rs. 5287, against Rs. 3591 for ST counterpart. This difference may basically be ascribed to the quality of allotted land which was generally relatively poor in tribal areas. The average amount is, however, not that meaningful because the net gain varied considerably from farmer to farmer depending on the quality of land, availability of irrigation, types of input and the type of crop grown. The net gain was also not meaningful to a majority of ST farmers (77.5%) who themselves occupied the land, prior to the allotment. On the contrary, nearly half of them had to part away with some of their initial encroachment, and thus, lost that income. A wide variation of net income existed from village to village. For example, in the village Beelpur (Morena) which recorded the highest net gain, the allotted land had already been illegally sold to original encroachers and the allottees were only getting the wages and not the share in profit. In Satpiplya and Jattakhedi of Sehore district where the allotted land was highly productive, the SC allottees had to face stiff resistance from powerful encroachers who were not providing any work on their fields, and thus, they had to pay a high price for maintaining their possession. In some villages, e.g., Sanodha (Sagar) the allottees actually incurred a loss in the reporting year, while in village Ghugra (Mandla) the net gain was merely Rs. 807.

Perceived Social Consequences

In the rural area land is not just an economic asset, it also forms the basis of social prestige. Therefore, in the programme of land distribution to landless dalits, one of the inbuilt imperatives of the programme was that this step will go a long way in developing self-esteem and enhance social prestige of this under-privileged section of the society.

During group discussion it was attempted to know the perception of the allottees about the social consequences of the programme. Two questions for this were also included in the schedule. The result of the questions asked in the schedule is tabulated in Table 3.11.

Table 3.11 brings out that the perception about social consequences had been mixed one and varied significantly from situation to situation. Therefore, the average total percentages are not that meaningful. A significant difference was, however, noted between the tribal areas where the initial encroachers were tribals, than in those villages where the encroachment was got released from non-SC, ST and the land was distributed to the SCs. Among the tribal allottees who received *patta* on their own land which was once registered as encroachment, there was a general feeling of contentment which was expressed as follows :

(a) A sense of security developed in them due to legal entitlement of the land.

(b) They could now get loan on this piece of land.

(c) They could now make capital investment on that land without a fear that the land may be taken back by the government.

(d) Becoming land owner from land less increased their social prestige.

(e) They could bargain better spouse for their children and also higher bridal price.

V

Social Conflict

Nearly 50 per cent of those tribals who had to part away with some of their land, the feeling was different. Even though no serious clashes developed since in most cases land transfer from ST to ST and also from SC to SC was made to near relatives, a sense of bitterness developed and the relations became strained. The general feeling among such cases was that the step had created bitterness and strained family and social relations between the people of their own castes. However, those who were landless and received legal entitlement, the step any how helped them to build self-esteem and enhance their prestige in the society.

In villages where the quality of land was good and the encroachers were from powerful landowning castes, these encroachers were very sore about the programme since they were holding the land for many years and had made a good amount of investment on that land. These were the areas where serious

Table 3.11: Perception of the *Patta* Holders

Village Code	*District*	*Block*	*Sample Village*	*Household who Perceived that Due to Patta Distributed to Them ill Feelings Developed Between tham*	*Household who Perceived that Due to patta Their Prestige in Society was Enhanced (% of Allottees)*
1.	Dhar	Nalcha	Nai Baroda	Nil	60.0
2.	Dhar	Nalcha	Golarzhiri	18.7	43.8
3.	Hoshangabad	Bawai	Nagwada	80.0	60.0
4.	Hoshangabad	Bawai	Ganera	40.0	60.0
5.	Sehore	Sehore	Satpiplya	86.7	13.3
6.	Sehore	Sehore	Jattakhedi	100.0	Nil
7.	Ujjain	Ujjain	Karohan	6.7	93.3
8.	Ujjain	Ujjain	Panthpiplya	28.6	85.7
9.	Sagar	Sagar	Sanodha	100.0	100.0
10.	Sagar	Sagar	Gidwani	86.7	80.0
11.	Mandla	Mandla	Ghugra	26.6	53.3

(Contd.)

Table 3.11 *(Contd.)*

Village Code	*District*	*Block*	*Sample Village*	*Household who Perceived that Due to Patta Distributed to Them ill Feelings Developed Between tham*	*Household who Perceived that Due to patta Their Prestige in Society was Enhanced (% of Allottees)*
12.	Mandla	Mandla	Hridaynagar	-	-
13.	Shehdol	Suhagpur	Lalpur	-	46.7
14.	Shehdol	Suhagpur	Kotma	13.3	46.7
15.	Chhindwada	Chhindwada	Khunarjhiri	20.0	66.7
16.	Chhindwada	Chhindwada	Mujawarmal	6.7	60.0
17.	Morena	Ambah	Beelpur	73.3	80.0
18.	Morena	Ambah	Joha	46.7	Nil
			Total SC	64.7	58.0
			Total ST	10.1	46.5
			Grand Total	39.4	52.7

conflicts were reported. In many cases where the SCs had to forcefully negotiate due to their vulnerable position, the general feeling among them was that the programme was just a political propeganda and they were cheated. Those SCs who could hold the good quality land due to the initiative of the State or by their own assertion and mobilization, the programme had definitely improved their economic and social status but they had to pay a heavy price for this in terms of social boycott which resulted in loss of wages, frequent insults, insecurity, and a sense of fear and non-cooperation.

Conflict may be conceived as a universal phenomenon, a part of human society which exists in every sphere of life. Conflicts take place between individuals, organizations, groups, and countries. A conflict generally emerges whenever two or more persons seek to possess the same exclusive position, play incompatible roles or undertake mutually incompatible means for achieving their purpose.

In the sociological literature, though as a matter of fact, there is no consensus on the conflict theory, vast literature is available which seeks to explain specific aspects of this social phenomena. Sociologists have identified two broad areas of conflicts, i.e., Endogenous – arising within a society due to the process of social dynamics, distribution of desirables and conflict of values and Exogenous – arising between systems. Great scholars like Marx, Mills and Dahrendorf have viewed social conflicts as being structurally induced, with their roots imbedded in inequitable economic resources, power structure and privileges. In Indian society dalits, especially Scheduled Castes had been put on the lowest ladder and had been an exploited class, both socially and economically. Even after more than 55 years of independence the basic ethos of Indian caste structure has not yet completely changed. Especially in rural India the people of the upper castes who have long wielded power and strength traditionally but whose vested interests have been adversely affected due to introduction of the provisions of social justice, put various obstacles in the smooth transition so that their interest may be served longer. The rising atrocities on the people of Scheduled Castes are also viewed in the light of a new level of awareness and consciousness among them that has enhanced their aspiration and assertiveness which is not tolerated by the socially and economically dominant group.

Various studies on conflicts between the Scheduled Castes and non-Scheduled Castes, especially in villages show that most of them still occur within the frame of a structural boundary of castes. So far as the cause of these conflicts and atrocities is concerned, dispute over land has been at the root. In a study conducted by Prof. R.G. Singh (1997) (unpublished) in the Institute on the nature, magnitude and causes of atrocities over Scheduled Castes in Madhya Pradesh, dispute over land was found to be the most important cause.

The programme of the distribution of surplus *Charnoi* land to landless persons of the Scheduled Castes and Scheduled Tribes during the year 2002 also met with stiff resistance, especially in non-tribal arreas, where the encroachers were from dominant castes and the quality of land was good. Immediately in the sowing season of 2003 various such conflicts were reported in the newspapers, e.g. 24 dalits were injured and one killed in Satpiplya village of Sehore district on 1st July, 2003 (*Dainik Bhaskar* 7.7.2003), armed attacks on dalits were made in Kherkhedi village of Rajgarh district (*Rastriya Sahara* 6.7.2003), Patharia Jogan of Sagar district (*Nav Bharat* 6.7.2003), Janai village of Shivpuri district (*Rastriya Sahara* 5.7.2003). Incidence of murder were also reported in Betul (*Nai Dunia* 4.7.2003) and Guna districts (*Dainik Bhaskar* 11.7.2003).

Sehore district had been the most notorious district where maximum cases of atrocities and armed conflicts occurred after the land distribution programme. In this report the following four cases–studied from Sehore district, conducted by Mr. Maneesh Vyas, a M.Phil Scholar are being presented to know their genesis:

1. Village Satpiplya
2. Village Gokulpura
3. Village Phoolmogra
4. Village Jattakhedi

Case Study of Satpiplya

Satpiplya is a village with a population of 2500, located 8 km. from Sehore, 6 km. away from Bhopal–Indore road. The quality of land in the village, including the one which was distributed to SCs is very good. The groundwater availability in the village is also good. The dominant land–owning caste in the village is *Khati* which belongs to OBC. The land which was freed from encroachment was also in the possession of *Khaties*. The SCs, consisting of *Balai, Chamars* and *Basod* are generally landless labourers or own very small pieces of land. These are labourers and work on the fields of *Khaties*. Many SCs were found to get an annual amount of Rs. 8,000 to 10,000 for working in the fields of upper caste farmers. Besides wages as labourer, *balais* also worked as midwife and were paid remuneration for this work. SCs live in separate *basti* and they have no social contact with upper castes people. Politically, in recent years some young people from *Chamar* caste had got motivated and had a patronage from Congress which was the ruling party at the time of conflict. *Khaties* were mainly the supporters of BJP.

Under the land distribution programme 36 *pattas* were distributed, 31 to *Ahirwar* (*Chamar*) and 5 to *Balai*. The encroached land which was distributed to SCs was under cultivation by *Khaties* for more than 10 years and quite a good amount of investment had been made by them to make this land productive. Under the Dalit Agenda, the one time workers overnight became the land owners and this was the main bone of contention between the dalits and the *Khaties*. *Khati samaj* organized themselves and started putting pressure on the SCs to refrain them from tilling the allotted land and maintain the *status quo*. The *balais* actually did not occupy the land due to the fear of loosing wages and their fee for midwife work. However, the *Ahirwals* in the leadership of one Kishan Ahirwal, a dalit activist and Congress worker, organized themselves and started tilling the land. Basically this created a tense atmosphere and *Khaties* adopted various means to insult the *Ahirwals*. On June 30, 2003 when the SC families were returning from fields, the armed

Khaties in a organized way attacked them resulting in 32 injured people. Four of them were seriously injured, of whom the leader, i.e., Kishan Ahirwal died. The incidence attracted *Star News*, *NDTV* and *Doordarshan*, and thus, received a wide national coverage. The administration was mobilized and a number of cases were registered under atrocity act, compensation was distributed among the aggrieved and police protection was provided to enable the SCs to maintain their hold on the allotted land. Although with the protection of police the *Ahirwals* could maintain their occupation, they were subjected to social boycott and are not being employed by *Khaties* on their fields till today. *Balais* have unofficially returned their *patta*.

Case Study of Gokulpura

Gokulpura village is situated 15 km. away from Sehore and 7 km. inside from Amkheda, located on Bhopal–Indore bypass. The village is very small with a population of 350 only. The population is mixed one, consisting of 4 *Khati* familes, 2 *Raghuvanshi,* 12 SCs and the rest are Muslims. Being a small village the *panchayat* is formed by including five villages, namely, Gokulpura, Usmania Gram, Labikheda, Ulkura and Sorta.

During the land distribution programme conflicts were reported in the village, some people sustained injuries and criminal cases were registered. However, in the village Gokulpura, the story was different. Here the *Charnoi* land had been under encroachment with SCs of Gokulpura village. Since the encroached land was larger than the permissible limit, the surplus land was got released from SCs and was distributed to landless SCs. Due to technical reason only two SC families of Gokulpura were given *patta* while the remaining *pattas* were distributed among SCs of Sorta village, located 8 km. away. In Gokulpura the conflict was not between SCs and upper caste people, as was the case in Satpiplya. On the contrary, the Muslims and *Thakurs* of village Gopalpura sided with SCs and socially boycotted the SCs of Sorta who had come to take possession of land. A conflict occurred between the allottees of Sorta village with the village folk of Gokulpura. Thus, this was a inter-village conflict.

Case Study of Fulmogra

Fulmogra is a village situated 10 km. from Sehore, away from the main road. The village is a small one with a population of around 1500. The caste structure of the village is similar to other villages i.e., comprising *Brahmins*, *Thakurs* and *Khaties* who are the main land-owning castes. The Scheduled Castes are mainly agricultural labourers living in separate *basties*. The special feature of the village Fulmogra is those Muslim families who own land, and due to their criminal background and connection, have a dominant position in the villages. These Muslim families maintain good relations with upper castes people of the village.

Under the land distribution programme ten SCs were allotted *patta* of very good quality agricultural land. However, this land was under the control of Babu Khan, Naba Khan and Majeed Khan who were cultivating this land for many years, and due to their criminal record, no one in the village dared to antagonize with them. When the SCs went to till the land the Muslim owner abused them and drew them off, damaging their hired tractor. The Hindus of the village did not provide any support to the dalits, even the *Sarpanch* who himself was from SC, tried to protect his skin and did not attempt to take any risk. On the complaint made to administration SDM came to village and handed over the possession to the SCs and the owner was arrested. However, he acquired bail and returned to the village and again forcefully snatched the land. The SCs being powerless were helpless, and despite *patta* allotted to them, could not cultivate the land.

Thus, the conflict in the village was between SCs and powerful Muslim encroachers and not between SCs and upper caste Hindus. A similar case study of village Kolukhedi of Sehore district was conducted and reported by Prof. R.G. Singh of the Institute where the SCs who were allotted 51.35 acres of land, could not acquire the possession from dominant Muslim owners, in spite of the intervention of the administration. In the village Kolukhedi as soon as the hold of administration became weak, the SCs were attacked on September 21, 2001 by the armed miscreants belonging to the party of *Jamindars* in which five SCs were injured and two of them sustained serious injuries. The case attracted media. However, despite all hew and cry, the allottees could not cultivate the land.

Case Study of Jattakhedi

Situated 6 km. from Sehore town, the village Jattakhedi is a medium sized road side village. The caste composition is similar to village Satpiplya and nearly 50 per cent population belongs to *Khati samaj*. Besides *Khaties* the land owning castes are *Thakur* and Muslim. Scheduled Castes belong to *Balai, Chamar, Beldar* and *Mehtar* and reside in separate *basti* situated outside the main settlement. Scheduled Castes are land less labourers or marginal farmers and mostly work in the fields of Hindu upper caste people or Muslims.

The *Charnoi* land in the village which was distributed to 28 SCs was a good quality land and was under unauthorized possession for more than 25 years with *Thakurs, Khaties* and *Muslims*. All these owners joined together and filed different civil suits against the SCs in the civil court. All these were powerful persons and insisted that since the land was under their possession from the time of ancestors and they had made large capital investment on this land, they will not allow the SCs to take possession. When the *tehsildar* and SDM came to hand over the possession to SCs, conflict took place, dalits were abused, some arrests were made. Administration tried to solve the problem but as soon as police protection slacked down the SCs were not allowed to till the land in the pretext that till court cases are solved they could not enter the fields.

The Overview

On the basis of the above referred case studies, the reports of newspapers, and the group discussions conducted in sample village, the facts that emerged about the conflicts may be summarized briefly as under :

(i) Land is an important resource in villages and who so ever holds the land, even if it is an unauthorized occupation, will not like to easily part away with his occupation. Therefore, any attempt of the State to change the *status quo* naturally will lead to conflicts.

(ii) In the tribal areas in most cases the allottees were the encroachers, and therefore, there was no question of dispute. Even in those cases where a tribal had to part away with some of his land, in spite of this fact that this step gave rise to bitterness, no serious conflicts took place. Other collaborative reasons for lower number of disputes were that in most cases the surplus land under the encroachment with the tribal was given to his near relative and secondly, the quality of land also was not that good.

(iii) In the non-tribal areas the situation was different. In the rural areas the Scheduled Castes are still socially much degraded and are economically dependent on the dominant section of the society. In nearly half of the cases (as per sample) where the allotted land was either vacant government land or was under the possession of SC, conflict did not take place. However, wherever the encroachment was with the dominant community, irrespective of his caste or religion, the land distribution met with resistance, especially in those cases where the land was fertile and was under encroachment for many years.

(iv) It was also observed that in many villages, realising their vulnerable position, some SCs compromised and did not put their actual claim by accepting some gratification. However, where there had been an emergence of dalit leadership, together with the political backing of the Congress or BSP, serious clashes were reported between the SCs and the land owners. Even in cases where administration provided full support and cooperation to see that the SCs are able to hold their land, they had to undergo frequent insults and due to social boycott, were debarred from getting work in their own villages and nearby.

(v) In cases where allotment was made to SCs of other villages, inter-village conflicts were reported between SCs themselves.

VI

Findings and Recommendations

Summary of Findings

The findings of the evaluation study of the land distribution programme to landless labourers of the Scheduled Castes and Scheduled Tribes, launched by the State Government during 2002, may be summarized briefly as under :

(i) As per the guideline allotment had to be made only to persons belonging to SCs and STs, firstly, to landless persons of category I and then to category II. On this count no discrepancy was observed during the survey.

(ii) Some complaints were received to the effect that in some cases more than one *patta* was given to persons within one family, defying the definition of a landless family.

(iii) In the tribal area, in a majority of cases the allotment of *patta* had been made to the same person who was previously cultivating that land as an encroacher. Nearly half of them, whose encroachment was more than two hectares, had to part away with some of their land. However, mostly the allotment of this surplus encroached land was made to his near relative to avoid conflicts. Baring few exceptions, the tribal allottees were found to actually hold the land.

(iv) The situation with respect to SC allottees was found to be quite different than ST areas. Here in more than 90 per cent cases the previous owner was different and mostly the encroacher was from non-SC, ST category. Wherever the encroacher was from powerful land-owning caste, stiff resistance was reported . Especially in areas where the quality of this land was good and the encroacher was holding the land from many years, various types of pressures were exerted on the SCs to refrain them from actually tilling the allotted land. In such areas some allottees who had no power to antagonize with the powerful land-owners, did not actually occupy the land, after accepting some gratification. In Morena district there were also reports that the allotted land was unofficially sold on plain paper to the original encroacher.

(v) During group discussions, in 9 out of 18 villages it was complained by the dalits that some influential persons from non-SC/ST category were still holding the government land and their encroachment was either not reported by *patwari,* or due to their political pressure, no serious attempt was made to free that land for distribution. Instead some poor quality government land was shown as surplus and distributed.

(vi) A significant difference was noted between the SC and ST allottees with respect to land quality and fertility level of the *patta.* The quality of land in the ST areas was found to be relatively poor. In the case of SCs, wherever the government vacant land was allotted, it was generally of poor quality, while in cases where the land was got released from non-SC/ST, it was of very good quality.

(vii) As per the guideline, no one had to be allotted landless than 0.5 hectare. However, violation of this norm was noted in tribal villages where nearly one-fourth of *pattas* of the size of less than half hectare were found to have been distributed.

(viii) The problem of difficult access was found to be only amongst SCs, especially in villages where the encroachment had been got freed from powerful non-SC/ST owners and the land was fertile

(ix) The availability of irrigation was found to be generally very low. However, it varied from individual to individual. On those fields which were under encroachment by the same farmer for long period, irrigation facility had been created by him.

(x) Though openly only few stated that they had to pay some bribe to get the land, the general feeling among the villagers was that the programme of land distribution provided good opportunity for administration to make money.

(xi) The overall average annual net financial gain worked out to Rs. 4131 per household, without taking into account his own labour cost. It was found to be significantly higher for SC respondents, as compared to ST. This difference may basically be ascribed to the quality of allotted land, which was relatively poor in tribal area. The average amount is, however, not that meaningful because it varied considerably from person to person, depending upon the quality of land, availability of irrigation, type of input and the type of crops grown.

(xii) In the financial terms the net gain was not meaningful to a majority of ST farmers who previously held the same land as encroachment. On the contrary, nearly half of them had to part away with some of their encroachment, and thus, lost that income.

(xiii) Those SC households who received good quality land, freed from non-SC encroachment and could actually hold the land due to the initiative of the State or by their own assertion and mobilization, the financial gain was very significant. However, due to stiff resistance and social boycott they had to pay a heavy price in terms of loss of wages and frequent insults.

(xiv) The perceptive about the social consequences had been mixed one and varied significantly from situation to situation. It was quite different with respect to tribal and SC allottees. Among the tribal allottees who received *patta* on their own land which was once registered as encroachment, the general feeling of contentment was expressed because this step freed them from insecurity, enabled them to take loan and bargain better bridal price. However, those who had to part away with some of their land, the general feeling was that this step created bitterness among fellow beings of their own caste.

(xv) In the villages the non-SC/ST encroachers of *Charnoi* land were very sore about the programme and were not prepared to hand over the land because they were holding the land from their ancestral time and had made significant capital investment on that land.

(xvi) Many SC allottees who had to face stiff resistance from powerful landlords had a complain that the administration was not providing them necessary support and assistance.

(xvii) After the land distribution programme various conflicts were reported throughout the State. However, in the tribal areas where the encroacher was the tribal himself, there was no question of dispute. Even in those cases where the tribal had to put away with some of his land, in spite of the fact that this step gave rise to bitterness, no serious conflict took place. Poor quality of land and allotment of this encroachment to his near relative were found to be other collaborative reason for lower number of disputes.

(xviii) In the non-tribal areas the situation was different. In the rural areas the Scheduled Castes are still socially much degraded and are economically dependent on the dominant section of the society. In nearly half of the cases (as per sample) where the allotted land was either vacant government land or was under the possession of SC, conflict did not take place. However, wherever the encroachment was with the dominant community, irrespective of his caste or religion, the land distribution met with resistance, especially in those cases where the land was fertile and was under encroachment for many years.

(xix) It was also observed that in many village, realizing their vulnerable position, some SCs compromised and did not put their actual claim by accepting some gratification. However, where there had been an emergence of dalit leadership, together with the political backing of the Congress or BSP, serious clashes were reported between the SCs and the land owners. Even in cases where administration provided full support and cooperation to see that the SCs are able to hold their land, they had to undergo frequent insults and due to social boycott, were debarred from getting work in their own villages and nearby.

(xx) In cases where allotment was made to SCs of other villages, inter-village conflicts were reported between SCs themselves.

Conclusion

Land distribution programme under the Dalit Agenda is an example of a programme which in spite of good intention of the government and a bold step towards providing social justice to the weaker sections, could neither fulfil the desired expectations of the dalits, nor yield fruitful political gain for the then ruling party. The reasons for this may be stated as below :

(i) Land distribution programme was a widely publicized programme applauded as a leap forward toward its commitment to empower the weaker sections and the commitment of the then ruling party towards the weaker sections. The programme, therefore, generated high aspirations among dalits which turned into discontentment when it was realized that at ground level they had to face many barriers. On the other hand, a feeling was developed among non-SC/ST counterpart that government was snatching their land and distributing it to dalits, for political gain.

(ii) In operationalization of the programme this ground reality was not given proper weightage that the so called surplus *Charnoi* land was mostly under encroachment and was not freely available to the administration for distribution. Especially in the non-tribal areas all of the good quality agricultural land had been under unauthorized occupation for so many years with the dominant castes of the village and they had also made capital investment on it, and therefore, were not prepared to leave this land.

Looking to the vulnerability of SCs it would have much better if strong administrative action should have been taken to firstly get this land released and keep it under government control, at least for one year. The *pattas* should have been distributed only after all legal matters on this land were settled at the government level itself.

(iii) The study shows that the financial gain varied considerably from situation to situation and in most cases was not as per the expectation of dalits. In the tribal areas where most of the allottees were the encroachers, the *patta* meant only legal entitlement and there was no extra monitory gain, on the contrary, it was a loss to them who had to part away with some of their encroachment. For the SCs, wherever government land was allotted, it was of very poor quality and where it was of very good quality the clashes with dominant owners reduced the charm of financial gain. Unfortunately due to corruption at lower level a general feeling also developed that the programme provided opportunity to the revenue department functionaries to make money.

(iv) Allotment of *pattas,* especially to SCs, significantly increased their prestige as their status changed from land less to land owners. For the STs also who got legal entitlement on their preview encroachment, the programme was a welcome step because it freed them from insecurity, provided them with the opportunity of loan and better bridal pride due to enhanced status. The long term impact of the programme in terms of the process of social change would have been much better if the hindrances at the ground level would have been taken care of in the beginning itself.

(v) The study demonstrates that the people of the Scheduled Castes are still socially degraded and wherever the interest of the dominant group, irrespective of his caste and religion, is undermined by any policy measure of providing social justice, hindrances are created and the SCs are pressurized. The *status quo* is maintained if SCs do not exert their right, however, wherever young leadership has emerged among SCs, conflicts occur which necessitates strong and effective action from the State in favour of the weak.

Recommendations

1. In spite of lapses in the execution of the programme which resulted in its low effectively, the programme in itself was a bold step towards providing social justice to the under-privileged, building in them a feeling of self-esteem and initiating a process of social change by empowering them. Therefore, it will not be desirable to consider it a political propaganda and put it in obliteration. In stead, in the second phase, it will be desirable to adopt a focused "Confidence Building Drive" and take up only those cases where the land was got freed from non-SC/STs and *pattas* were allotted, especially to SCs. All the problems regarding actual possession should be solved on the spot by taking strict administrative action. Wherever hindrances of any type are being created by dominant group, continuous vigilance be kept to ensure that the dalits keep on maintaining their right on their land. The help of a action group from dalits, constituted by the local administration, may be taken to see that their rights are not undermined in any way.
2. No effort should be made to dilute the cases of atrocity which occurred during the implementation of the programme. Sincere efforts must be made to send a message in the society that who so ever tries to put hindrances in the programmes aimed at providing social justice to weaker sections, will have to suffer serious consequences. Strong follow up action by the State in favour of weak is necessary for building confidence in them and start a process of social change.
3. To all the *patta* holders special financial assistance be provided for land development, irrigation, and for the purchase of necessary inputs so that the allotted land also proves to be a profitable asset.

4

Dalit Agenda and Charnoi Land Distribution among SCs and STs in Madhya Pradesh : Case Study of Dalits and Tribes of Bundelkhand Region

— *Yogesh Kumar**

and

— *Neha Chaturvedi***

Background

One of the primary reasons for widespread poverty amongst a large section of the scheduled communities is lack of access to iand and other natural resources. A small section of the community owns marginal landholdings, which are economically unviable and do not suffice their year long livelihood requirement. Being landless is the single most significant factor contributing towards their misery. In a country like India, where over 70 per cent of the population is still dependent on agriculture and its allied activities, ownership of land becomes a prerequisite to the survival of the people. With almost minimal alternative avenues for employment in the rural settings, rural population is dependent on agriculture for livelihood. Land thus becomes the prime source of livelihood for these people. Thus, ownership of land is the most essential condition for improving the existing living conditions in rural India.

With share of scheduled communities residing in the rural areas being significantly high, land ownership/entitlement becomes indispensable for their economic betterment. Government statistics reveal that though significantly high percentage of scheduled

* Director, Samarthan (NGO), Bhopal.

** Associated with Samarthan (NGO), Bhopal.

communities are dependent on agriculture and derive their livelihood from land, they are the most disadvantaged when land ownership pattern is taken into consideration. Incidence of landlessness is most pronounced among these groups. Landlessness is most pronounced in these communities, with agricultural labourer having marginal landholdings or sharecroppers comprising the bulk of this community.

Government data shows that majority of scheduled castes (about 77 per cent) and scheduled tribes (90 per cent) are landless and without any sustainable employment opportunities and productive asset (*Ninth Five Year Plan Draft, 1997-2002,* Planning Commission, Government of India). Around 87 per cent of the landholders of the scheduled castes and 65 per cent of the scheduled tribes in the country belong to the category of the small and marginal farmers (*Agricultural Census*, 1990-1992). According to the census, 64 per cent of scheduled castes and 36 per cent of the scheduled tribes main workers are agricultural labourers as against 31 per cent of the other communities. Also 25 per cent of the scheduled communities are cultivators compared to 40 per cent of the other communities and groups (*India*, 1992, Government of India Publication). Also the poorest amongst the poor are from these very sections of the society. As per the estimates of the Planning Commission, 48 per cent of the population of the scheduled castes and 51 per cent of the scheduled tribes are living below the poverty line.

It would not be wrong to say that given the socio-cultural setup of India especially the rural milieu, apart from the economic privileges that are associated with land and its ownership, social and cultural privileges and deprivations also revolve around ownership of land. Thus landlessness/poor land ownership position makes them vulnerable to all forms of social and economic exploitation. Time and again governments at both centre and state have made systematic endeavours (in terms of passing laws, issuing directives) to protect and promote the rights of these communities with regard to control and use of land but it has not been able to achieve its prophesied objective.

Land being a state subject adds another dimension to the adequacy of the legislations and directives that are issued from time-to-time, aiming at improvement of land ownership pattern amongst the communities. Due to land being a subject of the State List, the legislative and administrative responsibility in regard to land reforms, land distribution or any land related measure, rests with the state governments. Role of the Central Government is confined to merely laying down the general guidelines for implementation of the principals, keeping into view the socialistic ideology, which forms the basis of the Constitution of the country. Given this situation, variations are inevitable in the nature of legislative measures undertaken and their implementation. Besides, the role of socio-cultural factors along with political forces specific to the region cannot be denied as contributing towards differences in state policies on land.

The role played by the socio-cultural and political forces becomes significant primarily because of the feudalistic pattern of rural society. It is this feudalistic pattern that determines privileges and obligations due to a person, taking consideration of the strata of the society to which a person belongs. Scheduled castes and scheduled tribes comprise the lowest strata in social hierarchy and thus, meant to subserve other communities, higher in the social order. Given this setup, it becomes difficult to uplift the scheduled castes because any attempt by government to empower the community is resisted. It is resisted because it challenges the existing social order (of discrimination and domination) that has been in practice since times immemorial.

If we observe the land distribution pattern in India carefully, it is found to imitate the pattern of social hierarchy that we have discussed previously. As has been mentioned above, land is not valued for only its economic worth but is a socially valued asset too. Thus, its control and ownership affects the existing social pattern. In other words, its unequal distribution and control would serve to maintain and promote the hierarchical pattern of our society. It is a general observation that majority of large landowners belong to upper or the general castes while the agricultural labourers and workers are largely from scheduled community, mainly scheduled castes. In this light, we can understand that any initiative of the government that aims at fair distribution of land would be opposed as unequal land ownership pattern furthers the dominance of the upper castes.

Though cases of land alienation have been reported in many states like Madhya Pradesh, Andhra Pradesh etc., it widely acknowledged that a large number of such cases go unreported due to various reasons. Besides the influence of the above-discussed socio-cultural milieu, it is assumed that illiteracy and lack of awareness about land related laws could be an important contributing factor as a result of which such cases never come to light.

Ceiling of land and distribution of surplus land amongst the landless in scheduled communities would have improved the landholdings of these communities but it could not fulfil its objective. Large landowners evade ceiling through loopholes in the existing system like dividing the families on papers. Also in most of the states, ceiling limit is ascertained on the productivity of land, which gives ample scope to escape ceiling law. Determining the productivity of land or crop potential and categorization of land into different type provides ample scope to connive with the officials to evade land ceiling.

Also when it comes to benefiting from government schemes, it has been seen that due to lack of access to information and ignorance about the government procedures, scheduled castes are not able to benefit from the government schemes. There is no formal information dissemination mechanism existing in the rural areas. This role of information dissemination falls under the purview of *panchayats*, *panchayats* are largely defunct and thus do not serve the purpose.

Understanding the importance of land ownership in Indian society especially in the rural setup, initiatives have been taken by different governments to bring about a change in the lives of people hailing from scheduled communities–Scheduled castes and scheduled tribes. Realizing the importance that land has in the rural setting and the impact it has on the social status of people (besides economic value), the erstwhile government of Madhya Pradesh had taken a policy decision to distribute *Charnoi* land among landless from the marginalized communities. Time and again such initiatives have been proposed by the government for this section that is in utmost need of such assistance. **'Bhopal Declaration'** prepared by Madhya Pradesh Government, in its '21 point action agenda for 21st century' also categorically lays down the initiatives that the government proposes to undertake for upliftment of the tribals and the dalits.

Bhopal Declaration and *Charnoi* Land Distribution

Madhya Pradesh Government came up with Bhopal Document in the year 2002.This document was presented in Bhopal Conference (January 12-13, 2002) after which the final draft of the Bhopal Document was prepared. The conference also issued a **'Bhopal Declaration'** on the future of the Scheduled Castes and Scheduled Tribes of the nation.

Bhopal Document proposes a multi-dimensional approach for all-round development and upliftment of marginalized section–in terms of their empowerment through education, reservations in government sectors, protecting the rights of tribal, food security and likewise. A number of land related initiatives were also proposed in the document. These initiatives can be broadly seen under two heads :

A. *Initiatives Proposed for Scheduled Castes and Scheduled Tribes in the Unorganized Sector*

Meaningful intervention has to be made in the unorganized sector in order to bring about change in the lives of people from the marginalized communities.

1. *End landlessness*—As large sections of these communities are landless agricultural labourers, landlessness needs to be given high priority, which can be ensured by ending landlessness amongst this disadvantaged group. The following steps need to be undertaken :

   (a) *Redistribution of agricultural land*–Madhya Pradesh Government has already taken initiative where the state has decreased its area of grazing land from the mandatory limit of 7.5 per cent to 2 per cent in each village. This has led to a surplus of about 600 thousand acres, which is now being distributed amongst these communities.

(b) Creating material conditions by which scheduled castes and scheduled tribes landless labourers turn into sharecroppers to ultimately emerge into independent cultivators or to move to other occupation.

2. *Cultivators :* SC/ST cultivators are mostly marginal and small farmers. They lack infrastructural facilities and depend upon landlords for credit that leaves them vulnerable to all forms of exploitation. The state can come up with a series of policy packages based on the requirements of the cultivators from these communities.

B. Land and Land Reforms Proposed in Madhya Pradesh Model of Development

Reorganization of land-labour relationship has been given high priority in the Madhya Pradesh Model. Landless agricultural labourers form the largest category amongst the scheduled castes while they from the second largest category among scheduled tribes. Thus, any development model should address this issue on a priority basis. *Charnoi* land distribution is a beginning in this direction that aims to ensure that there are no people from these communities as landless agricultural labourers.

The previous Government of Madhya Pradesh had taken a policy decision to distribute *Charnoi* land among the scheduled communities as a welfare measure, aimed at bringing about a change in the lives of people belonging to the marginalized communities.

On 4th March 1998, the Madhya Pradesh Government issued a landmark Order asking all the district collectors to reduce the *Charnoi* land area from the existing 7.5 per cent of the total landmass reserved for grazing purposes to 5 per cent. On 19 September 2001, the State Government further reduced the *Charnoi* land from 5 per cent to 2 per cent.

Source : Bhopal Document

In the context of The Bhopal Declaration, the rationale for distribution of *Charnoi* land amongst this section of the society can be understood. The Bhopal Declaration, made in the Bhopal Conference (12-13 January 2002) puts forth various demands favouring the dalits. An important highlight of the declaration is the demand for ensuring that each dalit family owns enough cultivable land for socio-economic well-being. The government should pursue all possible measures including the distribution of surplus land, government land and temple lands. If need be, it should purchase cultivable land and distribute it amongst the dalits….. "One of the finest examples of this new endeavour is our recent decision to reduce the percentage of grazing/common land from 7.5 per cent to 2 per cent and thus allotting more than two-thirds of the total grazing land to SC/ST landless agricultural labourers." It has also been proposed in the document to create material conditions by which SC/ST landless agricultural labourers turn into sharecropper to ultimately emerge into independent cultivators.

As has been mentioned in the previous section, land ownership in India has social significance and is associated with social recognition and power. An initiative such as this (land distribution) would confer land ownership rights on the lower castes and is resisted by the upper castes. Incidences of violence have been reported from various parts of the state in the wake of *Charnoi* land distribution.

This paper is based on a research study 'Grazing Land to Dalits–Myths and Realities' carried out by *Samarthan*–Centre for Development Support, an NGO working in Madhya Pradesh and Chhattisgarh. The study was carried out during the year 2003-04. The study attempts to understand the issue of land rights of the dalits and the tribals in the backdrop of *Charnoi* land that was distributed amongst the marginalized sections of the society, the scheduled castes and the scheduled tribes. *Charnoi* land distribution took place in several rounds in Madhya Pradesh in the 1990s uptill the last Congress rule in the state. Though understanding the status of *Charnoi patta* holders is an important aspect of the study, the scope of the study permits us to analyze the issue of land and landlessness in its multiple dimensions. The issue of land rights of women is one such important aspect of the study where an attempt is made to understand provisions for women in different acts and policies like Madhya Pradesh Land Revenue Code, Hindu Succession Act or policy initiatives taken by government in order to ensure women ownership of land (Madhya Pradesh State Policy for Women). It also highlights other relevant issues like land encroachment (*kabzaa*), experiences of civil society organizations working on land rights (a case study of Ekta Parishad), role of *gram sabhas* and government officials in land distribution besides others.

The study aims to understand how effective *Charnoi* land distribution has been for the landless from the scheduled communities and the extent to which people have benefited from it. It also brings into focus the efforts that need to be made so that beneficiaries actually benefit from land distribution. In other words, how to make land distribution more effective and fruitful?

This paper presents the key highlights along with the conclusion and recommendations that were proposed in the study in order to ensure that marginalized section truly benefit from such government initiatives like distribution of land. One of the underlying objectives of the study was to enable the civil society actors in advocating the issue of land rights of Dalits and Tribals at the higher levels – state and national and in initiating dialogue with government to bring about favourable policy changes. Furthermore, it was anticipated that the findings of the study would be of assistance to voluntary organizations in providing a wider understanding on issues of land rights and the intricacies involved therein and would facilitate organizations working for the cause of land rights of the marginalized in carrying forward their struggle.

Background of the Study

A need was felt to carry out a study on land rights of scheduled castes and scheduled tribes to understand the issue of landlessness in its various dimensions focusing on the status of beneficiaries of *Charnoi* land distribution. The significance of land ownership in rural India can be understood in the context of the hierarchical structure of our society where roles are predefined on the basis of the community to which a person belong. Any attempt, which is not in consonance with the existing social hierarchy is not readily acceptable. Any attempt that adversely affects this social hierarchy is resisted with vengeance. Distributing land to the marginalized section is one such attempt that is not in consonance with the social rural set up. Incidences of violence and atrocities on the deprived communities have occurred in many places where land had been distributed among the dalits and the tribals. The study aims to analyze how effective land distribution has been for the landless and the extent to which people have benefited from it. The objective of land distribution is not reduction in the number of landless on papers. In light of the *Charnoi* land distribution, the study attempts to highlight the efforts that need to be made in order to mainstream the marginalized communities and to make land distribution more effective and fruitful.

Methodology

It is a sample study carried out in 8 villages of 2 district of Bundelkhand region of Madhya Pradesh, namely, Damoh and Panna. One block was identified from each of the district. From district Panna, block Shahnagar was selected and from Damoh, block Hatta. Keeping into mind the sensitivity of issue of land distribution, most of the villages were those where member organizations of Ekta Parishad are active or have a presence.

Table: 4.1: *District and Village wise Distribution of Land*

District	*Village*	*Patta Holders Interviewed*		
		Scheduled Castes	*Scheduled Tribes*	*Total*
Damoh	Ghogra, Udaipura, Badkheda, Bhidari	29	21	50
Panna	Khamtara, Beejakheda, Kachauri, Patpari	68	64	132
	Total	**97**	**85**	**182**

Purposive sampling technique was used for conducting the study, both for selecting the villages and the sample population for the study. Individual interviews and group discussions were conducted for data collection. Individual interviews were conducted with those who have been allotted land in distribution. Focused group discussion were conducted with different stakeholders mainly with women who have received joint *patta* in *Charnoi* land distribution, landless people in the villages, people who have encroached land for cultivation and mixed group of men and women. These group discussions were conducted with the purpose of understanding efficacy of land distribution and peoples' perspective on a wide range of issues in relation to land. Discussions were also held with the *patwaris*, in their capacity as field level revenue officers, to know their viewpoints on the whole process of land distribution.

Questionnaires were framed for conducting individual interviews as well as focused group discussions. Quantitative information was collected during the individual interview, which was then supported by qualitative information collected during the group discussions. This quantitative information was analyzed using Statistical Package for Social Sciences (SPSS).

In all, 182 *Charnoi patta* holders were interviewed in the two districts–50 respondents in Hatta block of Damoh district and 132 *patta* holders in Shahnagar block of Panna district. On the whole, 97 *patta* holders were from scheduled caste communities while the remaining 85 were from scheduled tribes.

For the purpose of conducting individual interviews, the sample comprised the beneficiaries, people who had received *Charnoi* land. Besides these individual interviews, focused group discussions were also conducted with different groups like

- Women and men who have received *patta* of *Charnoi* land (combined patta).
- Women and men from landless families of other communities.
- People who have made encroachments (*kabzaa*) on government land.
- Mixed group of men and women on issues of land rights.
- Navrachna workers.

Discussions were also held with people who received land in the earlier land distribution initiatives of the state government, prior to *Charnoi* land distribution. Focused discussions were also held with the *patwaris* of the respective villages in order to obtain information on government's point of view.

Ground Realities of *Charnoi* Land Distribution

Findings of the study reflect the status of *Charnoi* land distribution as has been found in the 8 villages, which were covered in the study and do not reflect upon overall land distribution that has taken place in the 2 districts or in the entire state. The findings are based on the quantitative information gathered from 182 respondents from the 8 villages that were surveyed. In this section, combined findings of both the districts have been presented.

- Only about 4.4 per cent respondents in both the districts have received some assistance from the government, both in financial and material form.
- 3.5 per cent cases have been found where both father and son living together have been issued *pattas* and where son is below 18 years of age.
- Till the time of the study, *patwaris* had not demarcated the distributed land in about 21 per cent cases.
- About 8 per cent cases have been reported where *pattas* of allotted land had not been issued.
- Cases have been found in which the beneficiaries have been distributed land in 2 and in few cases in 3 separate chunks.
- In only 49 per cent cases, copies of the map of allotted land and that of *khasara* have been given.
- About 61 per cent of the respondents have been given the *Bahi Khattas* of the allotted land.
- In about 24 per cent cases, people are no longer in possession of allotted land.
- About same number of people have not been given the possession of allotted land, about 26 per cent.
- About 4 per cent land distribution has been made in the name of women, mostly widowed.

Major Findings of the Study

A. Anomalies in Land Distribution Under Landless Categories 1 and 2

Category 1 : People not owning an iota of land nor is there any probability of their inheriting it.

Category 2: People who own upto 2.5 acres of land.

- Till the time of the study, land distribution had been made only under category 1 of landless in Hatta block (Damoh district). However, about 4 per cent such cases were found where beneficiaries belonged to category 2 of landless.

Case Study 1

In the same village Ghoghra (District Damoh), land allotment had been made under category 1 only till the time the study was carried out. However, another exception to the provision or in other words, an anomaly was found when the kotwar of the village who has been allotted land in the earlier round of land distribution, about 7 acres has again been allotted land during *Charnoi* land distribution. His son who he is les than 18 years of age and lives with his father has also been allotted land, though as per provision of category 1 of landless, he is not eligible (he would inherit land in future).

- In Shahnagar block (Panna district), land distribution has already been made under category 2 where about 7 per cent *Charnoi patta* holders had bought land prior to *Charnoi* land allotment.

- In the 4 villages of Shahnagar, 33 per cent respondents had inherited land. Five per cent owned 4-5 acres land when *Charnoi* land was distributed.

- About 17 per cent respondents in Shahnagar have been allotted only upto 1 acres of land including 2 cases where ½ acre of land has also been distributed.

- 3.5 per cent cases have been found where both father and son living together have been issued *pattas* and where son is below 18 years of age.

    (a) 4 per cent such cases have been reported in Ghoghra village in Hatta block (District Damoh).

    (b) 3 per cent cases have been reported in village Beejakheda Shahnagar block (District Panna).

Case Study 2

In village Ghoghra, people reported that the ex-*sarpanch* of the village, 'Harprasad Adivasi' whose wife is the current *sarpanch* of the village, has inherited land from his father. Harprasad has a brother too. 'Parhas' and land has been amongst the two brothers. Harprasad has a son 'Durpad' who is not yet married and lives with his father. He has been allotted land in the current round of land distribution. According to the provisions and the rules of *Charnoi* land distribution, his son is not eligible under category-1 of landless, under which all land distributions have been made in the village till date (till the time of the study). People expressed the opinion that when he can get *patta*, there are many like him in the village who are equally eligible. As Durpad falls under category 2 of landless, so do others have not been given patta on the ground that they would inherit their fathers land and such people are not being considered landless at present. People opined that *sarpanch* managed to get *patta* for his son because of his clout. Also, for all practical purposes, he is still the *sarpanch* (*sarpanchpati*).

B. Aid/Assistance from Government

- In both the districts combined, only 4.4 per cent respondents have received some financial assistance while about 9 per cent (which includes those who have received financial assistance too) have received non-monetary assistance.

  (a) In the 4 villages of Hatta block (Damoh district), none of the *patta* holders received any assistance in cash or kind from government.

  (b) It is only in village Khamtara (Shahnagar block) that 6 per cent beneficiaries have received some financial assistance from government, Rs. 800 and in another 12 per cent cases (which includes 6 per cent who have received financial assistance too), beneficiaries have received assistance in kind from the government. They have been distributed wheat in proportion to the size of the land allotted.

(*Note:* However, Government provision is of granting assistance to the tune of Rs. 3000 per hectare of allotted land mainly in kind to each *Charnoi* beneficiary.)

C. Findings on Issuing of Documents (Patta, Bahi Khata, Khasara and Plot Map) of the Allotted Land

- In 21 per cent cases, *patwaris* have not yet demarcated the distributed land.
  - (a) In Hatta block, 44 per cent people do not know where or which land has been allotted to them.
  - (b) Situation is better in Shahnagar, where land has not been demarcated in 3 per cent cases. (Those figures have not been included where forestland has been allotted and officials prevented the *patwari* from demarcating the land. Status of land thus allotted is unclear.)
- In one of the villages in Shahnagar block, Patpari, out of the 18 persons who were identified as landless and eligible for land allotment in early March 2001, *pattas* have so far been issued to only 22-24 per cent of them. Remaining beneficiaries have not been given even the *pattas* of the land. The *patwari* opines that the *pattas* are issued from the *tehsil* and he is in no way associated with issuing of *pattas*.
- In 49 per cent cases, copies of map of allotted land and that of *Khasara* have been issued to the *Charnoi* land beneficiaries.
  - (a) In Hatta block, copies of map of allotted land and that of *khasara* have been given to 56 per cent of the *patta* holders that were interviewed.
  - (b) In Shahnagar block, the same have been given to only 46 per cent respondents.
- Likewise, '*Bahi Khatas*' or '*Bhoo Adhikaar Pustikaa*' have been given to only 61 per cent of the respondents in all.
  - (a) 42 per cent people in the villages of the Hatta block have been issued '*Bahi Khatas*' or '*Bhoo Adhikaar Pustikaa*'.

(b) In Shahnagar, about 68 per cent respondents have been issued the Bahi Khattas.

D. *Termination/Removal from Allotted Land*

- About 24 per cent of the *patta* holders are no longer in possession of the distributed land.
  (a) In Hatta block, 36 per cent have lost possession over distributed land.
  (b) In the villages of Shahnagar too, 21 per cent respondents are no longer in possession of allotted land.
- 26 per cent cases have been found where people have never been given possession over allotted land in the 2 districts.
  (a) 44 per cent cases where people have not been given possession of their land have been found in Hatta block.
  (b) About 20 per cent such cases have been reported in Shahnagar block.
  (c) In Hatta block, it has been found that from amongst those people who are no longer in possession of the allotted land, 40 per cent cases are due to intra-community conflict while remaining 60 per cent cases are a result of inter-community differences, due to hold of other communities on land that has now been distributed. The reasons for loosing ownership of allotted land in Shahnagar and Hatta are more or less the same.
  (d) In village Bejaakheda of Shahnagar block, people have been allotted *pattas* for forestland, which they have been asked to vacate. About 77 per cent of the respondents who have lost possession on their land in Shahnagar block is due to the above mentioned factor.
  (e) Government indifference has been stated as the main reason for having not been given possession on allotted land in both Hatta and Shahnagar block. People have stated negligence and carelessness of government officials as the main reason for their plight. In few cases, due to the hold of upper caste on the allotted

land, few people have so far never taken possession of the allotted land but such cases are insignificant.

E. Previous Status of Distributed Land (which has Implications for Charnoi Patta Holders)

- In all, about 25 per cent respondents have been allotted land that has been previously been encroached (under *kabzaa*) by others.

(a) In Hatta block, 38 per cent respondents were such who have been allotted land that was encroached by others prior to its distribution (while in another 18 per cent cases; they have been allotted vacant surplus government land).

(b) In Shahnagar block, 21 per cent respondents have been allotted land that had previously been encroached by others. However, about 11 per cent *patta* holders have been allotted land, which was under their possession prior to its distribution.

(c) Out of the 38 per cent cases of allotment of land that was under others possession, only 37 per cent of the encroachers released or vacated the land on their own while in about 11 per cent cases, government pressure had to be applied to restore the land to the beneficiaries in Hatta block.

(d) Out of these 21 per cent cases in Shahnagar, only about 36 per cent have removed their claim from the land while the remaining 64 per cent have still not vacated the land, in some cases not even under government pressure.

(e) In Shahnagar block, only 11 per cent of the respondents who had encroached land have been allotted the *pattas* for the same while 12 per cent have stated that *pattas* for land they had been cultivating have been issued to others.

(f) In all the above-mentioned 12 per cent cases, *pattas* for encroached land have been allotted to others, from the same community and not to them, which has increased the possibility of intra-community violence.

F. *Other Findings*

- Combined/joint *pattas* have been issued in all villages except in village Khamtara (Shahnagar block). According to the patwari, *pattas* in the village had been issued before the decision on issuing joint *pattas* for *Charnoi* land was passed by the government. This is however wrong because the decision on issuing joint *patta* for every government land had been taken in the late 1980s and is effective since then.
- Except for village Kachauri (Shahnagar block) and Bhidari (Hatta block), where about 4-5 women knew that joint *patta* had been issued, remaining were ignorant about it.
- On the whole, awareness amongst men on joint *patta* is also negligible due to their being largely illiterate.
- No change in the status of the women or the families to whom *pattas* have been allotted mainly due to lack of awareness about their stake in the allotted land as well as due to poor quality of the land allotted with no likelihood of economic benefits in future. However, land ownership singly cannot lead to empowerment of women, it should not be looked upon in isolation.
- Lack of transparency on determining eligibility of landless especially where land has been allotted under category 2 of landless. This is mainly because *gram sabhas* are not held regularly (as has been found in village Badkhedaa, Hatta block) while in the rest, *gram sabhas* are held regularly but on registers, in absence of the required quorum.

Conclusions

On the basis of the findings of the study and its analysis, following inferences have been drawn in regard to the issues of land rights in the context of the study.

1. Much disparity has been found in *Charnoi* land distribution under both the categories of landless 1 and 2. In some region, land had been distributed only under category 1 while in some, under category 2 as well. Even where land distribution has officially been made under category 1 only,

instances of land allottment under category 2 have also been reported.

2. No uniformity in the implementation of the directives guiding land distribution under category 2. No clear information available on the guidelines determining what is the limit upto which if a person owns land, he can or cannot be considered eligible for land distribution. Furthermore, how much land would be distributed to individuals having different sizes of landholdings.

3. No clarity amongst the officials on who are to be considered or included under category 2 of landless which reflects in the manner of implementation of *Charnoi* land distribution orders.

4. Lack of awareness among people on who are landless in the eyes of government–who belong to category 1 or who would fall under category 2 or why they have/have not been considered eligible/not eligible for land distribution. There is widespread discontentment among people as a result of the above stated lack of awareness.

5. Allotment of *Charnoi* land will not automatically lead to improvement in the social, economic and financial status of the *patta* holders. In the villages studied, *Charnoi* land that has been distributed is by and large, wasteland that can never possibly be brought under cultivation. Barring few, most people are of the opinion that except for the satisfaction that ownership of land brings with it, they do not see any economic benefit from this land.

6. Development support fund has not been given to people and they do not have the resources to invest in land. Except in one village (village Khamtara, Shahnagar block) where some patta holders of scheduled castes communities were given Rs. 800 and some have been given wheat, rest nowhere, any assistance has been given to them. People do not have the resources to invest in land and thus, would not be able to start any agriculture related activity on the allotted land.

7. In considerable number of cases, people have not been given the necessary documents, supporting their ownership on the distributed land. There are cases where people have not yet been given the *pattas* of the allotted land. The question of receiving other documents does not arise.
8. Cases of people losing possession over allotted land have also been found in significant number of cases. The reasons have mainly been encroachment (*kabzaa*) on the same land by the dominant community and to some extent, encroachment by people of their own community. Allotment of forestland (Beejakheda village of Shahanagar block) has been a major cause, leading to peoples' losing control over allotted land.
9. Many people who have been allotted land have never been given possession over the land, supposedly allotted to them. There are many instances where the *patwari* has so far not measured/demarcated the land to the beneficiaries while in some cases, due to negligence of the officials, beneficiaries have not been able to take possession over the allotted land till the time of the study.
10. Another inference that reflects the futility of land allotment and general discontent is that the beneficiaries have not been allotted the land that was under their *kabzaa* (encroached) and which they have been cultivating for years now. This land is relatively better in quality as compared to the land that has now been allotted. If they were given legal possession over this land, it would have proved very beneficial.
11. Another issue related to the above is that with their having received land in current round of *Charnoi* distribution, they have lost eligibility for receiving land in future. With similar initiatives on land distribution in the future, they would ultimately lose the land that is presently under their *kabzaa* and on which they are dependent. Despite being a *Charnoi* land beneficiary, they would remain dependent on the land under their *kabzaa*.
12. Though violence has so far not been reported from these villages, possibility of violence remains high once people

start preparing their fields for sowing crops during July-August. Possibilities of both inter and intra community clashes remain high.

13. The process of identification of landless through the *gram sabha has* not been satisfactory. People are not content with the manner in which the landless were identified in the villages in the present round of *Charnoi* land distribution.

Recommendations

On the basis of first hand information collected from the field, during interactions with various groups of people in the village as well as with the government officials, academic and voluntary organizations, following recommendations have been proposed for making *Charnoi* land distribution more meaningful.

Short-term Recommendations

It includes such recommendations that require immediate notice and should be addressed at the earliest possible by concerned authorities.

- It has been found in the study that only in microscopic number of cases, people have been allotted *pattas* of that very *Charnoi* land, which they have been cultivating. Attempt should be made to ensure that people are assigned *pattas* for that very land, which they have been cultivating. Government provision states that *pattas* for encroached *Charnoi* land be issued to the person who is encroaching it, it needs to be enforced strictly.
- Assigning *patta* for encroached land would be beneficial because people have invested years, working hard in making it cultivable (which is besides the attachment that they have with it). If they are allotted some other land, it will again involve years of hard work in making the land cultivable. As *Charnoi* beneficiaries are mainly laborers and too poor to invest in land, how will their family survive, with no alternative sources of income to support them, if they work towards making the allotted land cultivable?

- There have been many instances in the villages surveyed where people have encroached 'other public land' in their villages, mostly *banjar* land and have been cultivating the same for years. They have now been given *patta* of *Charnoi* land. It is in the interest of these people that they be given the *patta* of that very land on which they have toiled for years, without considering if the land in question is categorized under the category of *Charnoi* land.
- Possession of BPL card should not be a criterion for granting Land Development Fund. *Charnoi patta* holders were not declared BPL in the survey last conducted and do not possess these cards. Therefore, all *Charnoi patta* holders should be declared BPL and eligible for their share of land assistance earmarked under BPL.
- *Patwaris* should be asked to submit details about landless as well as the status of available cultivable wasteland in the villages before distribution of land is initiated. These details should be made available to the *Tehsildars* and *Naib Tehsildars* well in time and it should be made mandatory. There appears to be a mismatch in government records and ground realities on the status of available cultivable wasteland and identified landless which has resulted in allotment of uncultivable land to beneficiaries.
- To make land distribution fruitful, it is essential to ensure that if encroached land (especially in cases where encroachment is carried out by other communities) is proposed for distribution, it is vacated prior to its allotment/ distribution. Administrative machinery should ascertain that there is considerable time gap between removal of *kabzaa* from the land and its reallotment. People should be warned of strict legal action in case of non-cooperation.

Long-term recommendations

- To streamline the whole process of land distribution and to make it transparent, first step that needs to be taken is to make *patwari naksha* of the village 'public'. *Patwari naksha* or village map contains details about total land available and its status in the entire village. How much land under various categories is available in the village etc. It also shows which land (under which *khasara* number) in the village belongs to whom and other detail like how much land in the village is encroached and the category to which it belongs. One such common place can be the *Panchayat* Bhawan where this map can be displayed for everyone. Putting up such information would increase transparency as well as awareness level amongst the people, avoiding unnecessary conflicts in the village. It also becomes important for determining ones eligibility on land, in cases of encroachment.

- Computerization of revenue records and easy access to receive such documents will enhance transparency and reduce corruption.
- As *Gram Sabha's* are not held regularly in the villages, there is a need for a more participatory process of identification of landless in the villages. People are not satisfied with the manner in which landless were identified in the villages in the current round.
- Systematic efforts need to be made by government at disseminating information/increasing awareness amongst people about *Charnoi* land distribution. This would help prevent widespread discontent amongst people. It would be beneficial for government and its officials that more transparency is maintained on the issues involved in land distribution, considering its sensitivity.
- A formal document stating the status of land holding of residents/natives of a village should be made public. Such a document is available with the *patwari*. This is relevant especially in those cases where land has been allotted under category 2 of landless–why and how much land has been allotted to a person? It would not only lend transparency to the whole process of land allotment, it would be easier to cross check the basis, on which land allotments have been made to one and all.
- Another suggestion that has been made with regard to encroached land is that like anti-encroachment drives undertaken in the cities, government should also restore to such steps in order to remove encroachments from

government land rather than imposing fine on people. Imposing fine can never prove to be a deterrent and can never prevent further encroachments. If people were not permitted to continue cultivating land by paying some fine, the question of resentment/clashes over allotment of one's encroached land to other would never arise. Anti-encroachment drive should be carried out on a regular basis as preventive measure.

- For the upliftment of marginalized section, different strategies need to be framed for different target groups, keeping in mind their traditional occupational pattern. Many communities in the villages are not involved in agriculture. Taking this into account, it becomes imperative that social and occupational structure of different communities be studied prior to deciding upon a uniform policy of land distribution. People from different communities have traditionally been involved in different professions. If alternative sources of income can be provided to them, it would be beneficial for them. One such example would be granting *patta* for ponds for fishing to people from fisher folk communities. Collective farming on government land where land is cultivated by people and its returns shared amongst them with inputs provided by government is another alternative besides other. Such alternatives have to be looked for because of limited availability of land, which cannot be given to all.
- A regular monitoring mechanism needs to be developed in order to ensure that people who have been allotted land are able to retain their possession on it and are able to cultivate it. A block-wise monitoring team needs to be formed to monitor the status of land ownership. Not only would it result in restoration of land in those cases where beneficiaries have been removed from allotted land, it would act as a check, leading to reduction/prevention such cases from taking place in future. The Task force should be strengthened more towards monitoring the land distribution/possession and publishing reports. Had such a system been evolved since the beginning of *Charnoi* land distribution started, drives like 'Operation Vishwas' would not have been required. Also,

drives such as Operation Vishwas would have been more effective if officials from Revenue Department are also involved in it.

- There is a need for quick legal redressal system in order to resolve issues of contention at the earliest possible, in relation with *Charnoi* land allocation. There is an urgent need for improvement in interdepartmental communication, between Revenue and Police department so that cases of land alienation can be prevented or resolved early.
- *Gram Nyayalayas* should be assigned special powers to take up and resolve issues of contention related to *Charnoi* land. As *Charnoi* land comprises the common property land of the village, such cases should be treated under the jurisdiction of *Gram Nyayalayas*, which should be directed to resolve such cases within the stipulated time.
- There should be clarity amongst the officials about the different directives framed by the government on *Charnoi* land. It has been found that there is uncertainty amongst the officials (especially amongst the *patwaris*) due to multiplicity of orders that have been issued in relation to *Charnoi* land. 3-4 orders have been issued in relation to *Charnoi* land so far. It should be ensured that with the announcement of every new policy or directive, previous orders are timely withdrawn and made ineffective. Also, it should be uniformly implemented in the entire state, at the same time.
- An attempt should be made by different organizations to come to a common understanding on how to work on land rights of marginalized. Different organizations have different abilities and strengths and together they can support/ Contribute towards the cause of the marginalized. Voluntary organizations can take up selected villages and provide long-term support to *patta* holders to enhance their skills and capacities to sustain their livelihood using the allotted land in most efficient manner. These models of economic and social empowerment will generate learnings for favourable policy changes to affect lives of a larger section of the poor dependent on land.
- Constant efforts need be made by actors of civil society working on the issue of land rights, to be able to substantiate

their views and opinions with concrete facts. Towards this end, research studies should be conducted, findings of which are more readily comprehensible and objective and which present a more clear and precise picture. Findings of such studies on different dimensions of land issues can then be shared at the larger level with government, both State and Centre, which could have policy implications.

- Civil society actors should make collective efforts at bringing the government to table and getting the issues resolved through dialogues and meetings. Civil society actors can together act as pressure group, which government would not ignore. However, in order to bring the voice of the *patta* holders on the table, sincere engagements on the issue of land is essential.

- Land rights to women–allotment of joint *patta* is imperative for upliftment of women and for giving them a place of honour in society but we cannot look upon land rights of women in isolation. It is a step, though very crucial towards women empowerment. In the direction of upliftment of women, it is essential that steps be taken by government to ensure other rights to women like *Political Rights* where in they can participate freely in political processes and raise their voice on issues of concerns in institutions of local governance, *gram sabhas* and *panchayats*, *Right to Education,* where girls have access to school and are not denied education on the basis of their sex, *Economic Rights*, where they are given equal wages for equal work or they are not denied work on the basis of their sex besides others. It is important for government to invest in social capital formation for generating critical awareness in the masses. Civil society organizations can play a major role in setting up some exemplary models of women empowerment by sensitizing and orienting both men and women. Some innovative pilot studies can also be taken up by voluntary organizations in order to highlight such cases of women empowerment where civil society has been working.

- There is an urgent need to sensitize media on *Charnoi* land 1distribution. Government has never taken any initiative to take media into confidence and has kept it in dark about the motives behind *Charnoi* land distribution. In such a state, media's role has been to a considerable extent critical and it reported facts as and when they occurred in regard to *Charnoi* land. Media can contribute immensely in furthering Government's objective of *Charnoi* land distribution but it has to be sensitized first, for which government has to take immediate steps.

The Road Ahead

With the Bhartiya Janta Party (BJP) coming into power in Madhya Pradesh in 2004, there is now a new government with its own developmental agenda, with its own set of priorities in the state. It has a peoples' mandate to fulfil that has led it to the corridors of power in the State.

The present government in the State had proposed a number of initiatives for the Scheduled Castes and Scheduled Tribes in its election manifesto. The Dalit Agenda of the previous government and the election manifesto of the present government show the commitment that the government's (both previous and present) have for the Scheduled Castes and Scheduled Tribes in the State. Though these are separate documents, the ultimate objective remains the same–upliftment of the marginalized sections of the society. However, the issue that arises here is—What fate the initiatives proposed by one government meet when it is no more in power? Are the policy decisions of one government left midway ones it is voted out of power? In the light of *Charnoi* land distribution, is it not important that we know what fate the initiative met after BJP was voted into office? Has the present government made attempts at following up with the *Charnoi* land distribution initiatives of the previous government?

The election manifesto of the present BJP government speaks besides others, distribution of land to landless labourers from the scheduled castes communities. It proposes to distribute 2 hectares of undisputed land to the family of landless labourer. It also promised to give Rs. 7000 to each of the family for land development and for buying agricultural implements. As regards, the scheduled tribes, amongst the many initiatives proposed are the ones that speak of granting them legal ownership over forestland under their *kabzaa*.

In the absence of information, it would not be appropriate to comment on the extent to which the present government has kept its commitment.

In the light of the above stated study, what fate do the people who were given the *patta* of *Charnoi* land meet, now that the Congress party has been voted out of power? What happens to the material and financial support that was assured to them? Has follow-ups been done on the present status of these *Charnoi* beneficiaries *vis-a-vis* possession and ownership of allotted land besides other areas of concerns as highlighted in the study? It is imperative for us to understand that initiatives like land distribution have both social as well as economic bearing. They need to be sustained over longer periods of time for the poor to be finally able to reap the benefits from the same.

It is crucial that we have a political environment in the State and the country where progressive initiatives of one government sustain irrespective of which party comes to power. Such initiatives should be above and beyond party politics. In the absence of such political backing/patronage, initiatives like *Charnoi* land distribution fade away into oblivion, into nothingness.

References

Government of M.P. (1995), *State Women Policy,* Bhopal.

Government of M.P. (2002), *The Draft Bhopal Document,* Bhopal.

Government of M.P. (2002), *Third Human Development Report,* Bhopal.

Jha, P. (2002), *Land Reforms in India: Issues of Equity in Rural Madhya Pradesh,* (ed.), New Delhi: Sage, Vol. 7.

Mander, Harsh, "Tribal Land Alienation in Madhya Pradesh". Working Paper Series No.13 published by National Centre for Advocacy Studies.

Michael, S.M. (1999), *Dalits in Modern India: Visions and Values*, New Delhi.

Mohanty. B.B. (2001), Land Distribution Among Scheduled Castes and Scheduled Tribes, *Economic and Political Weekly.*

Rajgopal, P.V. "Voice of Hope, Voice for Change" Working Paper Series No.18 published by National Centre for Advocacy Studies, Pune.

Ramagundam, Rahul (2001), *Defeated Innocence,* New Delhi, 2001.

Index